God's Purpose

Peter,

Thank you for retrieving my data.

Ron

God's Purpose
Ron Fredriks

Xulon Press

Xulon Press
2301 Lucien Way #415
Maitland, FL 32751
407.339.4217
www.xulonpress.com

© 2017 by Ron Fredriks

All rights reserved solely by the author. The author guarantees all contents are original and do not infringe upon the legal rights of any other person or work. The views expressed in this book are not necessarily those of the publisher.

Unless otherwise indicated, Scripture quotations taken from the King James Version (KJV)–*public domain,* the Holy Bible, New International Version (NIV). Copyright © 1973, 1978, 1984, 2011 by Biblica, Inc.™. Used by permission. All rights reserved, taken from the New King James Version (NKJV). Copyright © 1982 by Thomas Nelson, Inc. Used by permission. All rights reserved.

Printed in the United States of America.

ISBN-13: 978-1-54562-112-7

Table of Contents

Acknowledgments vii
Introduction ix

1	The Triune God	1
2	Satan's Role	4
3	The Fall, Then Grace	9
4	God's People	14
5	The Sacrificial Lamb	21
6	The Mediatorial Role of Christ	29
7	Salvation	35
8	The Old and the New Man	42
9	Faith	52
10	Suffering	60
11	Destiny	67
12	The Heart	70

Acknowledgements

This book would not be possible without those authors of the past whom God had given spiritual insight into various portions of scriptures. Those include: A. W. Pink, A. B. Simpson, F. B. Meyer, Charles Haddon Spurgeon, Jessie Penn-Lewis, Watchman Nee, Oswald Chambers, Matthew Henry and coauthors Jamieson, Fausset and Brown. I am also very much indebted to Laura Hawkins who edited and offered suggestions to make this more understandable.

Introduction

To avoid confusion and to live life with purpose, you would do well to understand who God is and what is he trying to achieve. Miss that, and you missed the point of why you are here. Understand what God is trying to accomplish, and open your heart to His leading, and you are on your way to harmonizing with God's purpose. The way to uncover His plan is to examine Scripture; everything else is just speculation. John, in John 20:31 (NKJV) says: "these are written, that you may believe that Jesus is the Christ, the Son of God; and that believing you might have life through His name."

Our life experiences and the Word go hand in hand in understanding what God is teaching us. The book of Proverbs is a collection of thoughts by Solomon and the unifying theme is that, "The fear of the Lord is the beginning of wisdom" (Proverbs 9:10 NKJV). Proverbs is a whetting of the appetite for wisdom and understanding as seen in Proverbs 2:1-5 (NKJV): "So son, if you receive my words, and treasure my commands within you, so that you incline your ear to wisdom, and apply your heart to understanding; yes if you cry out for discernment, and lift up your voice for understanding, if you seek her as silver, and search for her as for hidden treasures; then you will understand the fear of the Lord, and find the knowledge of God."

Solomon also wrote Ecclesiastes, which in good part was autobiographical. He pondered life's great questions, particularly the meaning of life, and came to the following conclusion: "Vanity of vanities. . . . all is vanity" (Ecclesiastes 1:2, 12:8 NKJV). After all the great things Solomon had done, he comes to the realization that life was empty, without permanent value, and only led to frustration. Solomon's solution to the whole matter: "Fear God, and keep His commandments; for this is the whole duty of man" (Ecclesiastes 12:13 KJV). Solomon knew and warned of the pitfalls of life and spoke of the folly of not developing the fear of the Lord. Solomon had a grasp of what true knowledge was and knew it did not come from intellectual endeavors but came when God opened our eyes to the truth. "Do not be wise in your own eyes; fear the Lord and depart from evil. It will be health to your flesh, and strength to your bones" (Proverbs 3:7-8 NKJV).

It is hard to understand why God put us in the situation we are in; we have a nature that falls short of pleasing Him, and we are susceptible to Satan, who tries to draw us away from Him. But as the truth is revealed more to us, we should begin to understand what God's purpose is in making us the way we are and to experience what it means to have "a closer walk with Him." 2 Peter 3:18 (NKJV) says: "grow in grace and knowledge of our Lord and Savior Jesus Christ" and as we grow in grace may we be given "the spirit of wisdom and revelation in knowledge of Him, the eyes of your understanding being enlightened; that you may know what is the hope of His calling, what are the riches of the glory of His inheritance in the saints" (Ephesians 1:17-18 NKJV).

The Bible cannot be understood by using natural wisdom as seen in 1 Corinthians 2:14 (NKJV): "But the natural man does not receive the things of the Spirit of God, for they are foolishness to him; nor can he know them, because they are spiritually discerned." As seen in Judges 21:25 (NKJV) there were times when the Israelites "did what was right in his own eyes" only to fail and be judged in their way of thinking. Solomon said in Proverbs 14:12 (NKJV): "There is a way that seems right to a man, but its end is the way of death." We cannot be guided in spiritual matters using our own opinions because of the simple fact that "My (God's) thoughts are not your thoughts, nor are your ways My ways, says the Lord. For as the heavens are higher than the earth, so are My ways higher than your ways, and My thoughts than your thoughts" (Isaiah 55:8-9 NKJV).

When you are able to see how the golden thread is being woven throughout history to achieve God's purpose you have gained wisdom. To have insight into why God allowed sin, Satan and suffering to enter the world, you have gained a better understanding of what God is doing to achieve His purpose. When you experience eternal security through Jesus Christ and the "faith of the Son of God" that He gives, you have gained great comfort. My hope is that as you study these various topics from Genesis to Revelation, you will gain much insight into God's purpose, or at the least, a whetting of the appetite for further study of His Word.

Chapter 1
The Triune God

Nature gives us a picture of God's creative ability, but does not give us much insight into the reason for such a creation. For more details on who God is and why God does what He does, we need to look at Scripture, especially His dealing and interaction with man; but before we do that, let us look at His creation.

"In the beginning God created the heavens and the earth" (Genesis 1:1 NKJV). God the Father, being the great Originator and Initiator, came up with this plan of creating the heavens and the earth. "The earth was without form, and void; and darkness was on the face of the deep. And the Spirit of God was hovering over the face of the waters" (Genesis 1:2 NKJV). Notice, "The Spirit of God" was hovering over the face of the waters, that part of God that imparts vital energy and action. This same Spirit can be seen throughout Scripture, an example seen in 2 Peter 1:21 (NKJV) when "holy men of God spoke *as they were* moved by the Holy Spirit." Holy men spoke as they were moved by the Spirit, by God Himself in spiritual form to communicate who He was, what He expected of man and then after Jesus was crucified, to indwell man with that same Spirit (John 14:16, 26, 15:26, 16:7).

In Genesis 1:26-27 (NKJV) God says: "Let Us make man in Our image, according to Our likeness, let them have dominion over the fish of the sea over birds of the air, and over every creeping thing that creeps the earth. So God created man in his own image; in the image of God He created him; male and female He created them." Of all the visible creatures He made in the previous verses of Genesis 1 we now see God creating man in the image and likeness of Him. Before we get swelled up with pride on this comment, try to understand that we are only an image or shadow of Him, for Christ only is the "express image of His person" (Hebrews 1:3 NKJV). The word "Us" signifies more than one person of the Godhead in making man. With the Son being the express image of God and the Spirit giving life we see a Trinity: the Father, Son and Holy Spirit all working in conjunction with each other to achieve His purpose. The Father being the great Architect or Originator of the plan, the Son carrying out His great design and the Spirit giving life to His creation. This trinity can be seen throughout the Bible and an example seen in Paul's closing remarks to the Corinthian believers: "The grace of the Lord Jesus Christ, and the love of God, and the communion of the Holy Spirit *be* with you all. Amen." (2 Corinthians 13:14 NKJV)

We know from Ephesians 1:11 (NKJV) that God works "all things according to the counsel of His will." His will being His good pleasure as seen in Isaiah 46:10 (NKJV): "My counsel shall stand, and I will do all My pleasure." He does as He pleases because it is His sovereign right to do so. There are various viewpoints on how far God goes to do all His pleasure, but listen to what Charles Haddon Spurgeon had to say in his sermon on Matthew 20:15.

> There is no attribute more comforting to His children than that of God"s Sovereignty. Under the most adverse circumstances, in the most severe trials, they believe that Sovereignty has ordained their afflictions, that Sovereignty overrules them, and that Sovereignty will sanctify them all. There is nothing for which the children ought more earnestly to contend than the doctrine of their Master over all creation—the Kingship of God over all the works of His own hands—the Throne of God and His right to sit upon that Throne.
>
> On the other hand, there is no doctrine more hated by worldings, no truth of which they have made such a football, as the great, stupendous, but yet most certain doctrine of the Sovereignty of the infinite Jehovah. Men will allow God to be everywhere except on

His throne. They will allow Him to be in His workshop to fashion worlds and make stars. They will allow Him to be in His almonry (residence) to dispense His alms and bestow His bounties.

They will allow Him to sustain the earth and bear up the pillars thereof, or light the lamps of heaven, or rule the waves of the ever-moving ocean; but when God ascends His throne, His creatures then gnash their teeth, and we proclaim an enthroned God, and His right to do as He wills with His own, to dispose of His creatures as He thinks well, without consulting them in the matter; then it is that we are hissed and execrated, and then it is that men turn a deaf ear to us, for God on His throne is not the God they love. But it is God upon the throne that we love to preach. It is God upon His throne whom we trust.

So "Whatever the Lord pleases He does, in heaven, and in earth, in the seas, and all deep places" (Psalm 135:6 NKJV). Now having established the fact that the triune God created all things and is on His throne to do what He pleases, the question is, what is He trying to achieve? Romans 8:28-29 (NKJV) tells us: "We know that all things work together for good to those who love God, for those who are called according to His purpose. For whom He foreknew, He also predestined to be conformed to the image of His Son." Miss that and you miss out on God's plan for you. Augustine wrote: "O Lord, Thou hast made us for Thyself, and our hearts are restless until they find their rest in Thee."

Chapter 2
Satan's Role

Not long after Adam and Eve were created, Satan appeared on the scene to tempt Eve. Many would question why God would allow this evil entity to tempt such an innocent victim, but He did. To help us understand more about Satan and his role in the fall of man, we turn to the writings of Jessie Penn-Lewis, coauthors - Jamieson, Fausset and Brown as well as the work of A. W. Pink.

> In Genesis we have the simple story of the garden, with the guileless pair unaware of danger from evil beings in the unseen world. We find recorded there Satan's first work as deceiver, and the subtle form of his method of deception. We see him working upon an innocent creature's highest and purest desires, and cloaking his own purpose of ruin under the guise of seeking to lead a human being nearer to God. We see him using the Godward desires of Eve to bring about captivity and bondage to himself. We see him using "good" to bring about evil; suggesting evil to bring about supposed good. Caught with the bait of being "wise," and "like God," Eve is blinded to the principle involved in obedience to God, and is *deceived* (see 1 Timothy 2:14).
>
> Goodness is, therefore, no guarantee of protection from deception. The keenest way in which the devil deceives the world, and the Church, is when he comes in the guise of somebody, or something, which apparently causes them to go God-ward and

good-ward. He said to Eve, "Ye shall be as gods," but he did not say, "and ye shall be like demons." Angels and men only knew evil when they fell into a state of evil. Satan did not tell Eve this when he added "knowing good *and evil.*" His true objective in deceiving Eve was to get her to disobey God, but his wile was, "Ye shall be like God." Had she reasoned, she would have seen that the deceivers suggestion exposed itself, for it crudely resolved itself into "disobey God" to be more like God!

(War On The Saints, Jessie Penn-Lewis)

Ever since men began to think and to speculate, the existence of moral evil under the government of a wise; holy, and benevolent Being has engaged the attention of intelligent and reflecting minds; but it is still an unsolved problem, and, notwithstanding the great scientific attainments of the present age, it probably will remain a mystery which will baffle the utmost efforts of philosophy to investigate.

Though made *perfect* in the full complement of his physical, mental, and moral powers, he was capable of being governed by the influence of motives; and being a voluntary agent in every thought, feeling, and act, he had to determine between the alternatives of following his own inclination or of bringing his will into complete subjection to the authority of God. Had he been a mere automaton, or a piece of inanimate matter, the Divine power might have been directly put forth to prevent his going out of his appointed sphere. But since he was a rational creature, placed under no stern necessity, but free to choose and to act for himself, it was morally impossible to prevent his fall. And how disastrous was that fall in its consequences! It may be supposed to have been easy for God to have overlooked, forgotten, or cancelled the first sin when it had been committed. But that is a superficial view of an offense which in its very nature severed the relations between the creature and his Creator, and, in the moral disorder of man's nature occasioned by it, brought into operation new agencies by which his condition was suddenly changed from a state of happiness to a state of misery.

(Bible Commentary, Volume 1,
Jamieson, Fausset and Brown)

Here for the first time in Scripture (Genesis 3) we meet with that mysterious personage the Devil. He is introduced without any word of explanation concerning his previous history. For our knowledge of his creation, his pre-Adamic existence, the exalted position which he occupied, and his terrible fall from it, we are dependent upon other passages, notably Isaiah 14:12-15, and Ezekiel 28:12-19. His (Satan's) chief aim is to get between the soul and God, to estrange man's heart from his Maker and inspire confidence instead, in himself. He seeks to usurp the place of the Most High to make his creatures his own willing subjects and children. His work consists of substituting his own lies in the place of divine truth. The method of Satan's approach was the same then as it is now. "Yea, hath God said?" He begins by throwing doubt on the Divine Word! He questions its veracity. He suggests that God did not mean what He had said. So it is today. By denying the Fall, the imperative need of the new birth has been concealed.

(Gleanings in Genesis,
A. W. Pink)

Paul warned us in 2 Corinthians 2:11 not to be ignorant of Satan's devices lest he get an advantage of us. Before Christ's death, Simon Peter, a very proud and self-confident disciple, told Jesus that no matter what happens he would be there for Him. In fact, Simon Peter said, "Lord, I am ready to go with You, both to prison and to death" (Luke 22:33 NKJV). But Jesus knew Simon Peter much better than he knew himself and replies: "Simon, Simon! Indeed, Satan has asked for you, that he may sift you as wheat; but I have prayed for you, that your faith should not fail; and when you have returned to Me, strengthen your brethren" (Luke 22:31-33 NKJV). Without an Advocate like Jesus, we also can be sifted as wheat; or in other words, to be tossed around in order to cause our faith to fail. After Peter's denial of the Lord (Luke 22:54-61), "Peter went out, and wept bitterly" (Luke 22:62 NKJV). Peter now knew what he was capable of doing in his own strength and must rely on the strength of the only One who could resist temptation, Jesus. Jesus used Satan so Peter would come to a realization of himself and from then on Peter was more aware of himself and how Satan works. Peter's life from then on is a strong testament to us of what it means to walk in the Spirit. Peter's words in 1 Peter 5:5-10 (NKJV):

> God resists the proud, but gives grace to the humble. Therefore humble yourselves under the mighty hand of God, that He may exalt you in due time, casting all your care upon Him, for He cares for you. Be sober, be vigilant; because your adversary the devil walks about like a roaring lion, seeking whom he may devour. Resist him, steadfast in the faith, knowing that the same sufferings are experienced by your brotherhood in the world. But may the God of all grace, who called us to His eternal glory by Christ Jesus, after you have suffered a while, perfect, establish, strengthen, and settle you. To Him *be* the glory and the dominion forever and ever. Amen.

Peter cast all his cares, temptations and fleshly desires upon Him and God gave Peter the wisdom and grace to overcome the evil one. Peter's ability to overcome the evil one after the crucifixion was because he now trusted in the strength of God to get him through life rather than trust in himself. God used Satan to perfect Peter into a usable and effective servant for Him. "To Him (not us) be the glory and the dominion forever and ever. Amen" (1 Peter 5:10 NKJV).

Paul's experience was similar who wrote the following words:

> And you He made alive, who were dead in trespasses and sins, in which you once walked according to the course of this world, according to the prince of the power of the air, the spirit who now

works in the sons of disobedience, among whom also we all once conducted ourselves in the lusts of our flesh, fulfilling the desires of the flesh and of the mind, and were by nature children of wrath, just as the others. (Ephesians 2:1-3 NKJV)

Chapter 3
The Fall, Then Grace

Adam and Eve were born perfect. Their lives were upright, not like ours, having a sin nature. Not having sin in their life gave them no barrier between them and their sin free God. God could have been satisfied with just innocent creatures like Adam and Eve for Him to commune with and worship Him, but He went a step further, allowing Satan to tempt them and them choosing to know good and evil. God could have protected them by giving them the grace not to believe Satan's lie but He did not, resulting in man now knowing both good and evil. We now see man in a very different and difficult situation, knowing good and evil, having an evil or sin nature that he cannot rid himself of. Before, he could walk in righteousness, but now he is powerless to walk in righteousness without divine grace, and that is the fallen position God wanted man in.

> The existence of sin in the world would afford a larger scope than any other for the exhibition of a new and unparalleled display of Divine benevolence. Accordingly, the announcement of a Deliverer was immediately consequent upon the fall of man (Genesis 3:15). The reign of grace commenced with the entrance of sin into the world; and thus the great scheme of mercy, by which, in a way would illustrate the glory of all His other perfections, God was to accomplish the restoration of the rebellious race, was not, as has been alleged, an after-thought, an expedient for repairing the failure of the Divine plan; for it had been designed in the councils of eternity,

and the world was prepared as the platform on which the destined interposition of divine love was to be manifested. In fact, this narrative of the fall, and the original promise and prophecy connected with it, form the basis of the whole religion of the Bible; and they are the principles of unity which make one consistent whole of the various dispensations of Providence. The patriarchal revelations, the call of Abraham, the promise made to him and his descendants, the Mosaic economy, the mission of the Hebrew prophets, and the introduction of Christianity, are each and all only separate parts, successive developments of one grand remedial scheme for the recovery of fallen man by the discipline of revealed religion and the merits of a Redeemer.

It remains only to notice that there is a striking correspondence between the close of the Bible and this opening portion of the sacred book. The objects that were withdrawn from view after the fall are reproduced upon the scene: paradise is restored, the ends of the sacred history are united, and the glorious circle of revelation completed. The tree of life, whereof there were but faint reminiscences in all the intermediate time, again stands by the water of life, and again there is no more curse. But a great advance has been made during the interval. Even the very differences of the forms under which the heavenly kingdom reappears are deeply characteristic, marking, as they do, not merely all that is won back, but won back in a more glorious shape than that in which it was lost, because won back in the Son. It is no longer paradise, but the New Jerusalem,—no longer the g*arden,* but now the *city* of God, which is on earth. The change is full of meaning: no longer the garden, free, spontaneous, and unlabored, even as man's blessedness in the state of a first innocence would have been; but the city—costlier, indeed, more stately, more glorious, but, at the same time, the result of toil, labor, and pain—occupied, not by a single human pair, but by a vast multitude. "whom no man can number,"—reared into a nobler and more abiding habitation, yet with stones which, after the pattern of "the elect corner-stone," were each, in his time, laboriously hewn and painfully squared for the places which they fill.

(Bible Commentary, Volume 1,
Jamieson, Fausset and Brown)

"Then the Lord God said, 'Behold the man has become like one of Us, to know good and evil' " (Genesis 3:22 NKJV). It appears what Adam and Eve did was a big mistake, but that was God's intention in order to make man more complete. God set about to have us know good as well as evil but God could not be implicated as the One who instilled evil, because God was not evil and had no evil. So He uses Satan as a tool, along with Adam and Eve's free choice to achieve His purpose to have them fall. They had a relationship with God but by disobeying God and believing Satan's lie they now had a relationship with Satan. "But your iniquities have separated you from your God; and your sins have hidden His face from you, so that He will not hear" (Isaiah 59:2 NKJV). We now have a wall between us and God because of the sin nature we inherited from Adam and the sins we commit daily. This wall can only be broken down by receiving Christ. "For if by the one man's offense death reigned through the one, much more those who receive abundance of grace and of the gift of righteousness will reign in life through the One, Jesus Christ." (Romans 5:17 NKJV) This is the key, we need Christ because our present state is as follows:

> As it is written:
> There is none righteous, no, not one;
> There is none who understand;
> There is none who seeks after God.
> They have all turned aside;
> They have together become unprofitable;
> There is none who does good, no, not one.
> Their throat is an open tomb;
> With their tongues they have practiced deceit;
> The poison of asps is under their lips;

> Whose mouth is full of cursing and bitterness.
> Their feet are swift to shed blood;
> Destruction and misery are in their ways;
> And the way of peace they have not known.
> There is no fear of God before their eyes.
>
> (Romans 3:10-18 NKJV)

So why would God go through all this trouble to bring sin upon man when He could have protected Eve from being deceived and Adam from making a wrong decision? F. B. Meyer explains: "human sin has been a path for God's glory, eliciting qualities in His love which otherwise had been unknown." God's gift to man was the freedom to think and the power to choose. We know good as well as evil and we can choose what direction we want to go. God wants us to realize the sinful state we are in and seek grace from Him to get out of our desperate situation.

Jesus says in Matthew 6:5 (NKJV): "And when you pray, you shall not be like the hypocrites", in other words, be humble in your sinful and desperate state. Jesus continues His instruction on prayer. "In this manner, therefore, pray:...Your (God's) will be done on earth as it is in heaven... And do not lead us into temptation, but deliver us from the evil one..." (Matthew 6:9-13 NKJV). God, who will do all His pleasure, wants you in this submissive, helpless and dire state so when deliverance comes, you will know what He has delivered you from and the grace and mercy He has given. God gives us a lifetime to figure this out and if you think you can get out of your position in your own strength, have at it — Satan is only too happy to help and encourage you in your quest.

> In every way that God can look at man, he is wrong and ruined, and the whole race lies condemned at the footstool of judgment.
>
> Finally, man is not only condemned, but utterly helpless ever to justify himself, or rise again into the favor of God: "Therefore no one will be declared righteous in his sight by observing the law; rather, through the law we become conscious of sin" (Romans 3:20 NIV).

Not only are we lost, but we can do nothing to save ourselves, and we are left absolutely at the mercy of God. God is very merciful in thus destroying our last hope of self-justification; just as the prisoner at the bar, if he cannot disprove the charges against him, is far wiser to plead guilty and throw himself on the mercy of the court. Now, this is the only way that God can ever interpose for the sinner. We have no rights by law, and if we claim any, we shall lose everything.

Now, this is the position that God wants to bring us to, where we shall cease our struggles and our attempts at self-defense or self-improvement, and throw ourselves helplessly upon the mercy of God. This is the sinner's only hope, and when he thus lies at the feet of mercy, Jesus is ready to lift him up and give him that free salvation which is waiting for all who are helpless enough to be willing to receive it.

This, too, is the greatest need of the Christian seeking a deeper and higher life, to come to a full realization of his nothingness and helplessness, and to lie down, stripped and stunned, at the feet of Jesus, as the apostle does in the seventh chapter: "What a wretched man I am! Who will rescue me from this body of death?" (Romans 7:24 NIV). Then shall he be able to answer in the joyful cry of the next verse, "Thanks be to God—through Jesus Christ our Lord!" (Romans 7:25a NIV). And the Savior's sanctifying power will come in all the fullness of the blessed chapter (Romans 8) that follows.

(The Christ in the Bible Commentary, A. B. Simpson)

Chapter 4
God's People

After the Fall, Adam and Eve were barred from the Garden of Eden and their good and easy life was exchanged for a life of hardship, by "the sweat of your face you shall eat bread" (Genesis 3:19 NKJV). Having evil, man and woman were now alienated from the life of God, but God's plan was to bring back that relationship as seen in Genesis 3:15 (NKJV). God's word to the serpent: "And I will put enmity between you (Satan) and the woman, and between your seed and her Seed (Christ); He (Christ) shall bruise your head (The crucifixion and finally when Satan will be cast into the bottomless pit (Revelation 20:2, 3)), and you (Satan) shall bruise His (Christ's) heel (Reference to the sufferings and death of Christ, "He was wounded for our transgressions, He was bruised for our iniquities" (Isaiah 53:5 NKJV)). From the book of Genesis we see how God's plan unfolds by using people like Noah, Abraham and Jacob.

The ark of Noah typified or foreshadowed salvation and it was covered inside and outside with pitch, which was a foreshadow of the Holy Spirit's seal or covering.

> Noah was commanded to construct the ark before a drop had fallen. So, too, the Saviorship of Christ was no afterthought of God when sin had come in and blighted His creation; from all eternity He had purposed to redeem a people unto Himself, and in consequence, Christ, in the counsels of the Godhead, was "the Lamb slain from the foundation of the world" (Revelation 13:8

KJV). The ark was God's provision for Noah as Christ is God's provision for sinners.

(Gleanings in Genesis,
A. W. Pink)

Through Abraham, God raises up the nation Israel and throughout their history, a promise of a Savior is to come (Isaiah 9:6-7, Isaiah 53:1-12, etc.). Of all the nations, Israel is "the apple of His eye" (Deuteronomy 32:10 NKJV). From Deuteronomy 32:11-12, we see how He watches over them through the ages: "As an eagle stirs up its nest, hovers over its young, spreading out its wings, taking them up, carrying them on its wings, so the Lord alone led him, and there was no foreign god with him" (Deuteronomy 32:11-12 NKJV). The progress of events are crucial in understanding what God is going to achieve, "an immutable purpose running through all the centuries like a golden thread, and reaching out to its final fulfillment in the coming ages" (A. B. Simpson).

This golden thread was always there, but not much light was given until the Savior came as seen in Romans 16:25 (NKJV): "Now to Him who is able to establish you according to my gospel and the preaching of Jesus Christ, according to the revelation of the mystery kept secret since the world began." Matthew Henry speaks of this mystery in his Bible Commentary: "During all times of the Old Testament this mystery was comparatively kept secret in the types and shadows of the ceremonial law, and the dark predictions of the prophets, which pointed at it, but so that they could not steadfastly look to the end of those things, 2 Corinthians 3:13. Thus it was hid from ages and generations, even among the Jews, much more among the Gentiles that sat in darkness and had no notices at all of it. Even the disciples of Christ themselves, before His resurrection and ascension, were very much in the dark about the mystery of redemption, and their notion of it was very much clouded and confused; such a secret was it for many ages."

Much is to be learned about God's purpose from Abraham's life. Abraham was promised a son and waited until he was 100 years old before Sara gave birth to Isaac. God said to Abraham in Genesis 22:2 (NKJV):

"take now your son, your only son Isaac, whom you love, and go to the land Moriah, and offer him there as a burnt offering on one of the mountains of which I tell you." God took the most precious thing in Abraham's life, his son Isaac and told him to sacrifice him. Scripture tells us when Abraham's knife was in the air, ready to sacrifice Isaac, God called out to Abraham to stop and said "now I know that you fear God" (Genesis 22:12 NKJV). While I am quite sure Abraham did not understand the significance of what he did at the time, it gives the picture of a future event when God would sacrifice His own Son for us. From this we see how Abraham's heart was tested in order to show where his true affections lay. Testing people was not something unusual for God to do, for He had previously tested, Adam, Eve, Cain, Abel and Noah as He will do with each of us. That is who God is and what He has intended to do as we live our life on this earth. Each trial or temptation is tailored by God for us. He knowing our limits and strengths will enable us to prove to Him, us, and the world, where our heart lies. God purposes us to go through the trial, and gives assurance in His Word that we can handle whatever comes before us as seen in 1 Corinthians 10:13 (NKJV): "No temptation (trial) has overtaken you except such is common to man; but God is faithful, who will not allow you to be tempted beyond what you are able, but with the temptation will also make the way to escape, that you may be able to bear it." Paul, who was constantly going through trials, opens our mind to the "why" of it in Hebrews 12:11 (NKJV): "Now no chastening (discipline) seems to be joyful for the present, but painful; nevertheless, afterward it yields the peaceable fruit of righteousness to those who have been trained by it." Notice, Paul calls this a training and elaborates more on this in Hebrews 12:12-14 (NKJV): "Therefore strengthen the hands which hang down, and the feeble knees, and make straight paths for your feet, so that which is lame may not be dislocated, but rather healed. Pursue peace with all people, and holiness, without which no one will see the Lord." Basically, God is building His army of believers who will see God and His purpose. God wants this army not only to be strong and bear fruit in this world, but to take on the forces of evil not only defensively but offensively, bringing praise and glory to His name. Luke 1:74-75 (NKJV) says: "To grant us that we, being delivered from the hand of our enemies, might serve Him without fear, in holiness and righteousness before Him all the days of our life."

Next we look at Jacob. From the beginning he was a confident, clever schemer and would not appear to be the person God would choose to work through to achieve His purpose. Jacob's brother Esau wanted to kill him (Genesis 27:41) after Jacob cheated him out of his birthright; so Jacob fled to protect himself. God did not have to chase Jacob away to teach him the lessons of life, Jacob flees to Laban because he does not have many alternatives after what he has done. Years later, after many trials and tribulations, Jacob has learned much through them and the lessons are coming to a climax. Jacob is now the head of a large family that is running low on food because of a great famine in the land and looks toward Egypt for help. As a side thought, God determined the great famine to happen to fulfill His purpose, even the putting in place of Joseph, Jacob's son, whom he presumes dead, to be the distributor of food. Jacob sending his sons, except the youngest Benjamin, to Egypt to acquire food is sent back to Jacob by the guardian of the stores, Joseph, whom they do not recognize. Simeon is held in Egypt and the other brothers are told to return with Jacob's youngest son. Jacob is now confronted with the decision to send Benjamin, his youngest and dearest son. Jacob's words in Genesis 42:36 (NKJV) to his children: "You have bereaved me: Joseph is no more, Simeon is no more, and you want to take Benjamin. All these things are against me." Jacob can no longer scheme his way out of this or use his natural strength as he once did, but is totally at God's mercy. Then the old and emotionally beaten Jacob says in Genesis 43:13 (NKJV): "Take your brother also, and arise, go back to the man and may God Almighty give you mercy before the man, that he may release your other brother and Benjamin. If I am bereaved, I am bereaved!" At this point God has achieved His purpose in Jacob; total frustration in himself to change the situation resulted in a total trust and submission to God. This took some time, as it will in our lives as well. Not only is Jacob changed, but history is moving in the exact direction God intended it to be. Jacob, whose name has been changed by God to Israel in Genesis 32:28, will go to Egypt with his whole family and be received as a highly respected person because of his son Joseph. As time goes on, Jacob's descendants will be held as slaves by the Egyptians and await God's deliverance. The golden thread being woven through history.

Now let us pass from Genesis to some 400 years after Israel's deliverance from Egypt to the life of David. As seen in 1 Samuel 16:13, Samuel the prophet anointed David as king even while Saul was king, which transpired because of Saul's disobedience. Proof of "the Spirit of the Lord came upon David from that day onward" (1 Samuel 16:13 NKJV) is shown by the great power and courage he had in his slaying of Goliath at a very young age, with only a stone and a sling (1 Samuel 17:49). David became a conquering and compassionate king, and also wrote many of the Psalms which express the yearnings of his heart. Here we may say to ourselves as we look at David's life after the anointing: "David is already there, his heart is in the right place, he has the Spirit of the Lord upon him, his road in life should be easy." The problem is, like us, is that he also had a sin nature that must be totally revealed and dealt with. David taking another man's wife and sending that man to the front of the battle certainly brought out the dark side of David. Not disciplining his son Absalom, resulting in Absalom taking over David's kingdom and later David allowing Absalom to live at the expense of David's loyal subjects was very dishonoring to David. When reading the Bible about David, you realize David paid dearly for those sins and it is a reminder for us to deal with our faults immediately and not allow them to get a hold of us and ruin the relationship we have with God. I am sure David could not imagine how a lax spirit on his part could produce such havoc and destruction. God achieved His purpose in David as seen in the Psalms when David spills out his heart to God in tears and repentance (Psalm 51). God having a purpose for David from the beginning continues His compassion toward him and his descendants eventually bringing forth the Savior through his lineage. The golden thread again being woven through history.

Now we move forward to Christ's time, and look at the life of Paul, formerly known as Saul. Saul "Circumcised the eighth day, of the stock of Israel, of the tribe of Benjamin, a Hebrew of Hebrews; concerning the law, a Pharisee; concerning zeal, persecuting the church; concerning the righteousness which is in the law, blameless" (Philippians 3:5-6 NKJV). Saul appeared to be at Stephen's trial (Acts 7:1-53) along with many other Jews including the high priest. Stephen preached the history of the Jews which included these final remarks to his audience: "You stiff-necked and uncircumcised in heart and ears! You always resist the Holy Spirit; as your fathers did, so do you. Which of the prophets did your fathers not persecute? And they killed those who foretold the coming of the Just One, of whom you now have become the betrayers and murderers, who have received the law by the direction of angels and have not kept it" (Acts 7:51-52 NKJV). Those were strong and incriminating words to the Jewish council. Jewish pride agitated by Satan who does not want the truth to surface, reacted: "they were cut to the heart and they gnashed at him with their teeth" (Acts 7:54 NKJV). The outcome was that Saul gave consent to have Stephen put to death. Saul being very motivated to crush this Christian sect, goes on and asks the high priest for letters which give him permission to bind those of the Way. On his mission to Damascus to bind those of the Way "a light shone around him from heaven. Then he (Saul) fell to the ground, and heard a voice saying to him, 'Saul, Saul, why are you persecuting Me?' And he said, 'Who are You, Lord?' then the Lord said, 'I am Jesus, whom you are persecuting. It is hard for you to kick against the goads (pricks or briars)' " (Acts 9:3-5 NKJV).

This incident reveals a few things about God when dealing with man. First, we see the compassion of God to reach down to someone who was killing His people and putting them in prison. Then notice in Acts 9:5 (NKJV); "I am Jesus whom you are persecuting." As Christians we have this same relationship with God as Stephen did, when we are wronged or persecuted it is as if they have wronged or persecuted Him. Then Jesus, who is the Lord, tells Saul; "it is hard for you to kick against the goads." (Acts 9:5 NKJV) In other words, you think you are important and on a powerful mission to help God but you are just beating your head against the wall in your warped understanding of the truth. God's irresistible Spirit has broken down Saul, with Saul asking "Lord, what do You want me to do?" (Acts 9:6 NKJV) This is also a perfect example of how God has chosen us for whatever reason, no matter how good or evil we are and not us choosing Him (John 15:16). We are not capable of seeing this truth unless it was revealed to us by God as seen in Romans 3:11(NKJV): "There is none who understands; there is none who seeks after God."

What have we learned from these personalities and the working of God in their lives? We have learned that if God chooses someone, no matter the personality, God will by His Spirit work through that person to have His way, while still preserving the personality of the individual. God not only works through His chosen vessels to achieve His purpose but through His enemies as well. For God will bend people to achieve His purpose. As Pharaoh was enslaving the Israelites in Egypt and not allowing them to leave Egypt, ten plagues came upon Egypt until Pharaoh agreed to let the Israelites go, only to change his mind later and pursue them. Pharaoh thought he was in the driver's seat but we are told in the Word that God hardened Pharaoh's heart to pursue after the Israelites. For it was God's purpose for Israel to escape as it was His purpose for the Egyptian army to be destroyed; "that the Egyptians may know that I am the Lord" (Exodus 14:4 NKJV). Not only is God's will done each day with his enemies, but in the end, Lucifer (or better known as Satan) will come to know the high hand of the Lord. "The Lord of hosts has sworn, saying, 'Surely, as I have thought, so it shall come to pass, and as I have purposed, so shall it stand: that I will break the Assyrian (Lucifer) (Isaiah 14:12) in My land, and on My mountains tread him underfoot. Then his yoke shall be removed from them, and his burden removed from their shoulders. This is the purpose that is purposed against the whole earth, and this is the hand that is stretched out over all the nations. For the Lord of hosts has purposed, and who shall annul it? His hand is stretched out, and who will turn it back?' " (Isaiah 14:24-27 NKJV)

Chapter 5
The Sacrificial Lamb

The words of Moses to the people of Israel in Exodus 11:4-7 (NKJV): Thus says the Lord: "About midnight I will go out into the midst of Egypt; and all the firstborn in the land of Egypt shall die, from the firstborn of Pharaoh who sits on the his throne, even to the firstborn of the female servant who is behind the hand mill, and all the firstborn of the animals. Then there shall be a great cry throughout all the land of Egypt, such as was not like it before, nor shall it be like it again. But against none of the children of Israel shall a dog move its tongue against man or beast that you may know that the Lord does make a difference between the Egyptians and Israel." A devastating tragedy for the Egyptians who had their own way to worship god but an unacceptable way. It is the same for all nations and religions of the world today. Acts 4:12 says: "Nor is there salvation in any other, for there is no other name under heaven given among men by which we must be saved." As Israel is held in bondage by the Egyptians, God reveals to Israel, as well as the Egyptians, what redemption is all about and what is needed to appease a Holy God "for all have sinned and fall short of the glory of God." (Romans 3:23) A. W. Pink in his book "Gleanings in Exodus" explains how the sacrificial lamb is a type or pattern of the "Lamb of God who takes away the sin of the world" (John 1:29 NKJV).

Exodus twelve records the last of the ten plagues. This was the death of the firstborn, and inasmuch as death is "the wages of sin", we have no difficulty in perceiving that it is the question of

SIN which is here raised and dealt with by God. It is true that God had purposed to redeem Israel out of Egypt, but He would do so only on a *righteous basis*. Holiness can never ignore sin, no matter where it is found. When the angels sinned God "spared them not" (2 Peter 2:4). The elect are "children of *wrath* even as others" (Ephesians: 2:3 KJV). God made no exception of His own blessed Son: when He was "made sin for us" (2 Corinthians 5:21)—He spared Him not (Romans 8:32).

But all of this only seems to make the problem more impossible of solution. The Israelites were sinners: their guilt was irrefutably established: a just God can "by no means clear the guilty" (Exodus 34:7 KJV): a sentence of death was passed upon them (Exodus 11:5). Nothing remained but the carrying out of the sentence. A reprieve was out of the question. Justice *must* be satisfied; sin *must* be paid its wages. What, then? Shall Israel perish after all? It would seem so. Human wisdom could furnish no solution. No; but man's extremity is God's opportunity, and He did find a solution. "Where sin abounded, grace did much more abound" (Romans 5:20 KJV), and yet grace was not shown at the expense of righteousness. Every demand of justice *was* satisfied, every claim of holiness *was* fully met. But how? By means of a *substitute*. Sentence of death *was* executed, but it fell upon an innocent victim. That which was *"without* blemish" died in the stead of those who had *"no* soundness" (Isaiah 1:6 KJV) in them. The "difference" between the Egyptians and Israel was not a moral one, but was made solely by the blood of the paschal lamb! It was in the blood of the Lamb that mercy and truth met together and righteousness and peace kissed each other (Psalm 85:10).

The whole value of the blood of the paschal lamb lay in its being a type of the Lord Jesus—"Christ our Passover is sacrificed for us: therefore let us keep the feast" (1 Corinthians 5:7-8 KJV). Here is Divine authority for our regarding the contents of Exodus 12 as typical of the Cross-work of our blessed Savior. And it is this which invests every detail of our chapter with such deep interest.

May our eyes be anointed so that we shall be able to perceive some, at least, of the precious unfoldings of the truth which are typically set forth.

The first great truth to lay hold of here is what we are told in the 11th verse: "It is *the Lord's* passover" (Exodus 12:11 KJV). This emphasizes a side of the truth which is much neglected today in evangelical preaching. Gospellers have much to say about what Christ's death accomplished for those who believe in Him, but very little is said about what that Death accomplished *Godwards*. The fact is that the death of Christ glorified God if never a single sinner had been saved by virtue of it. Nor is this simply a matter of theology. The more we study the teaching of Scripture on this subject, and the more we lay hold by simple faith of what the Cross meant to God, the more stable will be our peace and the deeper our joy and praise.

The particular aspect of truth which we now desire to press upon the reader is plainly taught in many a passage. Take the very first (direct) reference to the "Lamb" in Scripture. In Genesis 22:8 (KJV) we read that Abraham said to his son, "God will provide Himself a lamb for a burnt offering." It was not simply God would "provide" a lamb, but that He would "provide *Himself* a lamb." The Lamb was "provided" to glorify God's character, to vindicate His throne, to satisfy His justice, to magnify His holiness. So, too, in the ritual on the annual Day of Atonement, we read of the two goats. Why *two*? To foreshadow the two great aspects of Christ's atoning work —Godwards and usward. "And he shall take the two goats and present them before the Lord at the door of the Tabernacle of the congregation. And Aaron shall cast lots upon the two goats; one lot *for the Lord,* and the other for the scapegoat" (Leviticus 16:7-8 KJV). It is *this* aspect of truth which is before us in Romans 3:24-26 (KJV), "Being justified freely by His grace through the redemption that is in Christ Jesus. Whom God hath set forth to be *a propitiation* through faith in His blood to declare *His righteousness* . . . that He might be *just,* and the justifier of him which believeth in Jesus." In 1 Corinthians 5:7 (KJV) we read, "Christ *our* Passover." He is now *our* Passover, because He was first *the Lord's* Passover (Exodus 12:11).

Now there are two lines of thought associated with *sacrifices* in Scripture. First, a sacrifice is a propitiatory satisfaction rendered unto God. It is to placate His holy wrath. It is to appease His righteous hatred of sin. It is to pacify the claims of His justice. It is to settle the demands of His law. God is "light" as well as "love." He is of "purer eyes than to behold evil, and canst not look on iniquity" (Habakkuk 1:13 KJV).

Here, then, is the primary thought connected with "sacrifice." It is a bloody offering to appease the holy wrath of a sin-hating and sin-punishing God. *And this* is the very word which is used again and again in connection with the Lord Jesus the Great Sacrifice. Thus, Ephesians 5:2 (KJV): "Christ also hath loved us, and hath given Himself for us an offering and *a sacrifice to God* for a sweet-smelling savor." Again, "Once in the end of the world hath He appeared to put away sin *by the sacrifice* of Himself" (Hebrews 9:26 KJV). And again, "This man, after He had offered one *sacrifice* for sins forever sat down on the right hand of God" (Hebrews 10:12 KJV). The meaning of these passages is explained by Romans 3:25, 26: Christ was unto God a "propitiation", an appeasement, a pacification, a legal satisfaction. Therefore could the forerunner of the Redeemer say, "Behold the Lamb of God which taketh away the sin of the world" (John 1:29 KJV).

The second thought associated with "sacrifice" in the Scriptures is that of *thanksgiving and praise* unto God; this being the effect of the former. It is because Christ has propitiated God on their behalf that believers can now offer "a sacrifice of praise" (Hebrews 13:15 KJV). Said one of old, "And now shall mine head be lifted up above mine enemies round about me; therefore will I offer in His tabernacle *sacrifices of joy*" (Psalm 27:6 KJV). Said another, "I will sacrifice unto Thee with a voice of thanksgiving" (Jonah 2:9 KJV). This is why, after being told that "Christ our Passover hath been sacrificed for us" (1 Corinthians 5:7 KJV), the exhortation follows "therefore let us keep *the feast*" (1 Corinthians 5:8 KJV). The paschal lamb was first a sacrifice unto God; second, it then became the food of those sheltered beneath its blood.

The ritual in connection with the Passover in Egypt was very striking. The lamb was to be *killed* (Exodus 12:6). Death must be inflicted either upon the guilty transgressor or upon an innocent substitute. Then its *blood* was to be taken and sprinkled upon the door-posts and lintel of the house wherein the Israelites sheltered that night "Without *shedding* of blood is no remission" (Hebrews 9:22 KJV), and without *sprinkling* of blood is no salvation. The two words are by no means synonymous. The former is for *propitiation;* the latter is faith's *appropriation.* It is not until the converted sinner *applies* the blood that it avails *for him.* An Israelite might have selected a proper lamb, he might have slain it, but unless he had *applied* its blood to the outside of the door, the Angel of Death would have entered his house and slain his firstborn. In like manner today, it is not enough for me to know that the precious blood of the Lamb of God was shed for the remission of sins. A Savior *provided* is not sufficient: he must be *received.* There must be *"faith* in His blood" (Romans 3:25 KJV), and faith is a *personal* thing. I must exercise faith. I must by faith take the blood and shelter beneath it. I must place it between my sins and the thrice Holy God. I must rely upon it as the sole ground of my acceptance with Him.

"For I will pass through the land of Egypt this night and will smite all the firstborn in the land of Egypt, both man and beast; and against all the gods of Egypt I will execute judgment; I am the Lord. And the blood shall be to you for a token upon the houses where ye are; and when I see the blood I will pass over you, and the plague shall not be upon you to destroy you, when I smite the land of Egypt" (Exodus 12:12, 13 KJV). When the executioner of God's judgment saw the blood upon the houses of the Israelites, he entered not, and why? Because death had already done its work there! The innocent *had died* in the place of the guilty. And thus justice was satisfied. To punish twice for the same crime would be unjust. To exact payment twice for the same debt is unlawful: Even so those within the blood-sprinkled house were secure. Blessed, blessed truth is this. It is not merely God's mercy but His *righteousness* which is now on the side of His people. Justice itself *demands* the acquittal of every believer in Christ. Herein lies the glory of the Gospel. Said the apostle Paul, "I am not ashamed of the Gospel of Christ; for it is the power of God unto salvation to every one that believeth; to the Jew first, and also to the Greek" (Romans 1:16 KJV). And *why* was he not "ashamed" of the Gospel? Hear his next words, *"For* therein is *the righteousness of God* revealed from faith to faith."

"And when I see the blood I will pass over you." God's eye was not upon the house, but on the blood. It might have been a lofty house, a strong house, a beautiful house; this made no difference; if there was no blood there judgment entered and did its deadly work. Its height, its strength, its magnificence availed nothing, if the blood was lacking. On the other hand, the house might be a miserable hovel, falling to pieces with age and decay; but no matter; if *blood* was upon its door, those within were perfectly safe.

Nor was God's eye upon those within the house. They might be lineal descendants of Abraham, they might have been circumcised on the eighth day, and in their outward life they might be walking blamelessly so far as the Law was concerned. But it was neither their genealogy, nor their ceremonial observances, nor their works, which secured deliverance from God's judgments. It was their personal application of the shed blood, and of that alone.

"And the blood shall be to you for a token upon the houses where ye are; and when I see the blood, I will pass over you" (Exodus 12:13 KJV). To the mind of the natural man this was consummate folly. What difference will it make, proud reason might ask, if *blood* be smeared upon the door? Ah! "The natural man receiveth not the things of the Spirit of God: for they are *foolishness* unto him" (1 Corinthians 2:14 KJV). Supremely true is this in connection with God's way of salvation—"For the preaching of the cross is to them that perish *foolishness;* but unto us which are saved it is the power of God . . . But we preach Christ crucified, unto the Jews a stumbling-block, and unto the Greeks foolishness" (1 Corinthians 1:18, 23 KJV). It is faith, not reasoning, which God requires; and it was faith which rendered the Passover-sacrifice effective; "Through *faith* he kept the Passover, and the sprinkling of blood lest he that destroyed the first-born should touch them" (Hebrews 11:28 KJV).

In Isaiah, the long awaited Messiah was prophesied to come as the Sin-Bearer "He was led as a lamb to the slaughter" (Isaiah 53:7 NKJV). Hebrews 9:26 (NKJV) speaks of Jesus as this Redeemer, "but now, once at the end of the ages, He has appeared to put away sin by the sacrifice of Himself."

God's purpose for instituting the Passover was to show Israel and the world what was needed for deliverance and redemption. When the Passover is observed today, emphasis is not put on the blood as it should for Hebrews 9:22 (NKJV) says: "according to the law almost all things are purified with blood, and without shedding of blood there is no remission." For these animal sacrifices of the past were "patterns" (Hebrews 9:23 KJV), "but now, once in the end of the ages, He has appeared to put away sin by the sacrifice of Himself" (Hebrews 9:26 NKJV). Stephen was correct to reprimand the Jewish council for not seeing this truth and his words could very well apply today: "You stiffed-necked and uncircumcised in heart and ears! You always resist the Holy Spirit; as your fathers did, so do you" (Acts 7:51 NKJV). As Abraham was bringing Isaac to the mountain to be sacrificed, Isaac asked, " 'where is the lamb for a burnt offering?' and Abraham said, 'My son, God will provide for Himself the lamb for a burnt offering' " (Genesis 22:7-8 NKJV). How prophetic was Abraham's statement at that time. As "Abraham stretched out his hand and took the knife to slay his son" (Genesis 22:10 NKJV), the Lord told Abraham "Do not lay your hand on the lad" (Genesis 22:12 NKJV). "Now I know that you fear God, since you have not withheld your son, your only son, from Me" (Genesis 22:12 NKJV) "Then Abraham lifted his eyes and looked, and there behind him was a ram caught in a thicket by its horns. So Abraham went and took the ram, and offered it up for a burnt offering of his son" (Genesis 22:13 NKJV). A substitute was given to Abraham as it has been given to us. When John the Baptist saw Jesus coming he proclaimed: "Behold! The Lamb of God who takes away the sin of the world!" (John 1:29 NKJV)

Chapter 6
The Mediatorial Role of Christ

Let us begin by asking the question, Why did God ordain the office of priesthood? Wherein lay the necessity for it? The first and most obvious answer is, because of sin. Sin created a breech between a holy God and His sinful creatures. Were God to advance toward them in His essential character it could only be in judgment, involving their sure destruction; for He "will by no means clear the guilty" (Exodus 34:7 KJV). Nor was the sinner capable of making the slightest advance toward God, for he was "alienated from the life of God" (Ephesians 4:18 KJV), and thus, "dead in trespasses and sins" (Ephesians 2:1 KJV); and as such, not only powerless to perform a spiritual act, but completely devoid of all spiritual aspirations. Looked at in himself, the case of fallen man was utterly hopeless.

But God has designs of *grace* unto men, not unto all men, but unto a remnant of them chosen out of a fallen race. Had God shown grace to all of Adam's descendants, the glory of His grace had been clouded, for it would have looked as though the provisions of grace were something which were due men from God, because of His having failed to preserve them from falling into sin. But grace is *unmerited* favor, something to which no creature is entitled, something which he cannot in any wise *claim* from God. Therefore it must be exercised in a *sovereign* manner by the Author of it (Exodus 32:19), that grace may appear to be grace (Romans 11:6).

But in determining to show grace unto that people whom He had chosen in Christ before the foundation of the world (Ephesians 1:4, 2 Timothy 1:9), God must act in harmony with His own perfections. The sin of His people could not be ignored. Justice clamored for its punishment. If they were to be delivered from its penal consequences, it could only be by an adequate satisfaction being made for them. Without blood shedding there is no remission of sins. An atonement was a fundamental necessity. Grace could not be shown at the expense of justice; no, grace must "reign through righteousness" (Romans 5:21 KJV). Grace could only be exercised on the ground of accomplished redemption (Romans 3:24).

And *who* was capable of rendering a perfect satisfaction unto the law of God? Who was qualified to meet all the demands of divine holiness, if a sinful people were to be redeemed consistently with its claims? Who was competent both to assume the responsibilities of that people, and discharge them to the full satisfaction of the Most High? Who was able both to honor the rights of the Almighty, and yet enter sympathetically into the weakness and needs of those who were to be saved? Clearly, the only solution to this problem and the only answer to these questions lay in a *mediator*, one who had both ability and title to act on God's behalf and on theirs. For this reason was the Son of God appointed to be made in the likeness of sin's flesh, that as the God-man He might be a "merciful and faithful High Priest" (Hebrews 2:17 KJV); for *mediatorship* is the chief thing in priesthood.

(Exposition of Hebrews,
A. W. Pink)

The revelation of Jesus Christ reveals a greater and higher mystery (not known before) regarding mediatorship and fellowship with God. This revelation is that Christ, the sinless One, died in full obedience to His Father's will, shed his blood and took it as a sacrifice into the Heavenly Tabernacle and received God's complete acceptance and approval for the sins of mankind. Jesus has become for His people that believe on Him, our Great High Priest and Mediator, continually interceding for us and bringing the *very life of God* to indwell each of His believers (restoring their fellowship with Him) by the power of the Holy Spirit! He indeed is our Heavenly Leader and Forerunner, making possible what could not possibly be known under the Old Covenant (Old Testament Dispensation).

The glories of our Savior are set before us as our eyes are fixed upon Jesus. He is the Author and Finisher of our faith (Hebrews 12:2), and He is crowned with glory and honor in the heavens (Hebrews 2:9). The book of Hebrews, as well as other parts of scripture, bring out many important truths concerning Christ's mediatorial role as seen below.

> "God... spake" (Hebrews 1:1 KJV). Deity is not speechless. The true and living God, unlike the idols of the heathen, is no dumb Being. The God of Scripture, unlike that absolute and impersonal "first Cause" of philosophers and evolutionists, is not silent. At the beginning of earth's history we find Him speaking: "*God said,* Let there be light; and there was light" (Genesis 1:4 KJV). "He spake and it was done, He commanded and it stood fast" (Psalms 33:9 KJV). To men He spake, and still speaks. For this we can never be sufficiently thankful!
>
> "God who... in diverse manners spake" (Hebrews 1:1 KJV). The majority of the commentators regard these words as referring to the *various ways* in which God revealed Himself to the prophets—sometimes directly, at others indirectly—through an angel (Genesis 19:1, etc.); sometimes audibly, at others in dreams and visions. But, with Dr. J. Brown, we believe that the particular point here is *how* God spake *to the fathers* by the prophets, and not how He has made known His mind to the prophets themselves. "The revelation was sometimes communicated by typical representations and emblematical actions, sometimes in a

continued parable, at other times by separate figures, at other times—though comparatively rarely—in plain explicit language. The revelation has sometimes the form of a narrative, at other times that of a prediction, at other times that of an argumentative discourse, sometimes it is given in prose, at other times in poetry" (Dr. J. Brown). Thus we may see here an illustration of the *sovereignty* of God; He did not act *uniformly* or confine Himself to any one method of speaking to the fathers. He spake by way of promise and prediction, by types and symbols, by commandments and precepts, by warnings and exhortation.

"In these last days" (Hebrews 1:2 KJV). This expression is not to be taken absolutely, but is a contrast from "in time past." The ministry of Christ marked "the last days." That which the Holy Spirit was pressing upon the Hebrews was the *finality* of the Gospel revelation. Through the "prophets" God had given predictions and foreshadowings; in the Son, the fulfillment and substance. The "fullness of time" had come when God sent forth His Son (Galatians 4:4 KJV). He has nothing now in reserve. He has no further revelation to make. Christ is the *final* Spokesman of Deity. The written Word is now complete. In conclusion, note how Christ *divides history;* everything before pointed toward Him, everything since points back to Him. *He* is the *Center* of all God's counsels.

Christ is the irradiation of God's glory. The Mediator's relation to the Godhead is like that of the rays to the sun itself. We may conceive of the sun in the firmament, yet shining not; were there no rays, we should not see the sun. So, apart from Christ, the *brightness* of God's "glory" could not be perceived by us. Without Christ, man is in the dark, utterly in the dark concerning God. It is in Christ that God is *revealed*.

The Lord Jesus was not only the first in time, but the Chief, not only among but over them. In Romans 8:29 (KJV) we read, that God has predestinated His elect to be conformed to the image of His Son in order that He might be the Firstborn among many brethren, i.e., their Chief and most excellent Ruler. In Colossians 1:15 (KJV)

He is designated the "Firstborn of every creature," which most certainly *does not* mean that He was Himself the first to be created, as many today wickedly teach, for never does Scripture speak of Him as "the Firstborn of God," but affirms that He is the Head and Lord of every creature. In Colossians 1:18 (KJV) He is spoken of as "the Firstborn from the dead," which does not signify that He was the first to rise again, but the One to whom the bodies of His saints shall be conformed—see Philippians 3:21. In Hebrews 11:28 this term is applied to the flower and might of Egypt. In Hebrews 12:23 (KJV) the Church in glory is termed "the Church of the Firstborn." This title then is synonymous with the "appointed Heir of all things." It is, however, to be distinguished from "Only begotten" in John 1:18, 3:16 (KJV). This latter is a term of *endearment,* as a reference to Hebrews 11:17 shows—Isaac was not Abraham's *only* "begotten," for Ishmael was begotten by him too; but Isaac was his *darling;* so Christ is God's "Darling"—see Psalms 22:20, 35:17.

"Therefore, God, Thy God, hath anointed Thee with the oil of gladness" (Hebrews 1:9 KJV). The Spirit is still quoting from the 45th Psalm. The enemies of God's truth would discover here a "flat contradiction." In Hebrews 1:8 the One spoken to is hailed as "God," on the throne. But here in Hebrews 1:9 He is addressed as an inferior, "*Thy* God hath anointed Thee." How could the same person be both supreme and subordinate? If He Himself had a God, how could He at the same time be God? No wonder Divine things are "foolishness to the natural man!" Yet is the enigma easily explained, the seeming contradiction readily harmonized. The Mediator was, in His own person, both Creator and creature, God and man. Once we see it is *as* Mediator, as the God-man, that Christ is here spoken to, all difficulty vanishes. It is this which supplies the key to the whole passage. Much in Hebrews 1 cannot be understood unless it be seen that the Holy Spirit is there speaking not of the essential glories of Christ, but of His mediatorial dignities and honors.

(Exposition of Hebrews,
A. W. Pink)

Ephesians 2:18 (NKJV) says: "For through Him we both (Jew and Gentile) have access by one Spirit to the Father." Christ, in His meditorial role, unites all people to Him whether Jew and Gentile to make "one new man," (Ephesians 2:15 NKJV). This "new man" having no differences or contradictions, whether Jew or Gentile, is the man whom God can communicate with and have fellowship because His righteous indignation against their sin has been met. The words of 1 Peter 2:6-10 (NKJV) reveal God's character in the person and means He used to accomplish this.

> "Behold, I lay in Zion a chief cornerstone, elect, precious, and he who believes on Him will by no means be put to shame."
>
> Therefore, to you who believe, He is precious, but to those who are disobedient,
>
> "The stone which the builders rejected has become the chief cornerstone,"
>
> and
>
> "a stone of stumbling and a rock of offense."
>
> They stumble being disobedient to the word, to which they also were appointed. But you are a chosen generation, a royal priesthood, a holy nation. His own special people, that you may proclaim the praises of Him who called you out of darkness into His marvelous light; who were once not a people but are now the people of God, who had not obtained mercy but have now obtained mercy.

Chapter 7
Salvation

God's objective is that no one will perish, but all will come to a belief in Him and have eternal life. His plan of salvation is through belief in His Son, His only Son. God will also not be mocked by a lackadaisical, non-committal belief in His Son; for it needs to be a deep and everlasting commitment or else it just becomes a mockery. Paul said in Galatians 6:7 (KJV): "Do not be deceived, God is not mocked; for whatever a man soweth, that shall he also reap."

John 3:16 (KJV) says: "For God so loved the world that He gave His only begotten Son, that whoever believes in him should not perish but have everlasting life." A belief in Jesus for everlasting life sounds simple, direct and easy, but a shallow belief in such a passage could bring about a false sense of security. I do not want to diminish in any way what Christ did to take away sins and give eternal life, but I do want to bring it to light that if anyone does not see the true effectiveness of what Christ did for them, then they may be fooling themselves concerning eternal life. That is why it is important to make our call and election sure, a check and balance concerning our eternal security. We do not have Jesus here physically to test our motives but we can be like David who prayed, "Examine me, O Lord, and prove me; try my mind and my heart." (Psalm 26:2 NKJV)

The rich young man in Matthew 19:16-22 (NKJV) came to Jesus and asked Him "what good things shall I do that I may have eternal life?" Jesus could have said "he who believes in Me has everlasting life" (John 6:47 NKJV), but He did not. Instead, Jesus says, "if you want to enter into life, keep the commandments" (Matthew 19:17 (NKJV)), to which the rich young man replies, "Which ones?" Jesus lists six of them, to which the young man answers, "All these things I have kept from my youth. What do I still lack?" Up to this point the rich young man sounds as if he is very committed to do what the Jewish law required and if there is anything else he lacks he will follow. Jesus probes his heart further by saying "If you want to be perfect, go sell what you have and give to the poor, and you will have treasure in heaven; and come, follow Me" (Matthew 19:21 NKJV). "But when the young man heard that saying, he went away sorrowful, for he had great possessions" (Matthew 19:22 NKJV). The rich young man was tested on how committed he was, and we also will be tested as to our sincerity. When the rich young man met the Lord after his death, there should be no surprises to what would happen and why should it be any different for us.

    Let's look further into this issue of eternal life by examining another of Jesus' teachings. Many times, Jesus spoke in parables to give a picture of the point He was trying to get across. The parable in Luke 8:4-8 speaks of the sower, the seed and the soil and an explanation of the parable is given by Jesus in Luke 8:11-14 (NKJV). "Now the parable is this: The seed is the word of God. Those by the wayside are the ones who hear; then the devil comes and takes away the word out of their hearts, lest they should believe and be saved." This group was excited when first hearing about God's plan of salvation but the words did not make a lasting impression in their hearts. Next, "the ones on the rocks are those who, when they hear, receive the word with joy, and have no root, <u>who believe</u> for a while and in time of temptation fall away." So would you have eternal life if you are in this category, believed in the Lord Jesus Christ for a while? Hebrews 6:11-12 (NKJV) says "And we desire that each one of you show the same diligence to the full assurance of hope until the end, that you do not become sluggish, but imitate those who through faith and patience inherit the promises." There are others in this parable. "Now the ones that fell among thorns are those who, when they have heard, go out, and are choked with cares, riches, and pleasures of life, and bring no fruit to maturity." Knowledge and conviction did not save this group as it did not save the rich young man who was choked with the cares and riches of this life and never gained eternal life. Then we finally get to the ones Jesus is looking for. "But the ones that fell on the good ground are those who, having heard the word with a noble and good heart, keep it and bear fruit with patience." These are the ones who "keep it" and have a totally committed heart to follow Him. Jesus did not want half-hearted Christians, He wanted full-hearted ones.

But wait a minute, didn't Peter have a totally committed heart to follow Jesus and failed miserably as seen in Matthew 16:21-23 and Matthew 26:31-33, reprimanding and denying the Lord Jesus? Surely he failed, but God needed to test and show him what he was made of. As we grow in the good ground our old nature needs to be exposed, we need to be watered, enlightened to what spiritual life is. Even though Peter was whole hearted and diligent to serve the Lord, he never realized the subtle poison that existed within himself. Peter said in Matthew 26:33 (NKJV) "Even if all are made to stumble because of You, I will never be made to stumble." But we know Peter did reject Christ after the servant girl said "You also were with Jesus of Galilee." Peter, at this point in his life, did not know himself and what he was made of. The following is a good explanation of what natural man is.

> The natural man is born "like a wild ass's colt" (Job 11:12 KJV), completely unmanageable and self-willed, determined to have his own way at all costs. Having lost his anchor by the Fall, man is like a ship entirely at the mercy of winds and waves. His heart is unmoored, and he runs wild to his own destruction.
>
> (The Nature of God, A. W. Pink)

A Biblical description of natural man is found in Romans 3:10-12 (NKJV):

> There is none righteous, no, not one;
> There is none who understands;
> There is none who seeks after God.

> They have all turned aside;
> They have together become unprofitable;
> There is none who does good no, not one.

So how can we grow in good ground if our life is so deplorable and we are so totally depraved? The answer is that we must be drawn into Him to receive life and truth. John 6:44 (NKJV) says "No one can come to Me unless the Father who sent Me draws him; and I will raise him up at the last day." Even though we must be drawn by the Father to receive eternal life, it will be no excuse at the judgement for not receiving eternal life as was the case with the rich young man. He will be held accountable for not accepting what Christ required of him.

Eternal life is not received because "I will" to have eternal life, but because I am enlightened by Him to know the way of salvation. So if we go back to John 3:16 where it says "whoever believes in Him should not perish" the "whoever" are the ones the Father is drawing and growing in nourishing soil so they may be brought to maturity. It would be better understood as, "everyone that heareth," or everyone that believes and receives what God has revealed. If the "whoever" was anyone who willed salvation, then John 6:44 would be a contradiction. We cannot explain why some are drawn to Him and some not but we have to take what it says in the Bible as truth. If we have been drawn by Him we should be extremely thankful. There are many who are not concerned in the least about salvation and could be classified as the ones Jesus spoke of in Mark 6:6 (KJV) after teaching in the synagogue at Nazareth. "He marveled because of their unbelief."

Peter, the one that stumbled in the beginning wrote the words of 2 Peter 1:10-11 (NKJV). "Therefore brethren, be even more diligent to make your call and election sure, for if you do these things you will never stumble; for so an entrance will be supplied to you abundantly into the everlasting kingdom of our Lord and Savior Jesus Christ." So the one who stumbled in the beginning wrote "you will never stumble." Peter now had God's life in him, no longer operating in the flesh or natural life. Another great verse that brings out this growing process is John 15:4 (NKJV). "Abide in Me, and I in you. As the branch cannot bear fruit of itself, unless it abides in the vine, neither can you, unless you abide in Me." And then the tragic consequences of not abiding is seen in John 15:6 (NKJV), "If anyone does not abide in Me, he is cast out as a branch and is withered (no spiritual life); and they gather them and throw them into the fire, and they are burned."

Then one said to Him, "Lord, are there few who are saved?" And He said to them. "Strive to enter through the narrow gate, for many, I say to you, will seek to enter and will not be able. When once the Master of the house has risen up and shut the door, and you begin to stand outside and knock at the door, saying, 'Lord, Lord open for us' and He will answer and say to you, 'I do not know you, where you are from,' then you will begin to say, 'We ate and drank in Your presence, and You taught in our streets.' But He will say, 'I tell you I do not know you, where you are from. Depart from Me, all you workers of iniquity.' There will be weeping and gnashing of teeth, when you see Abraham and Isaac and Jacob and all the prophets in the kingdom of God, and yourselves thrust out." (Luke 13:23-28 NKJV).

As you can see, there is much to be concerned about and a false sense of security would be disastrous, but it is possible for believers to feel secure in their faith. God does not want our minds to be in an indeterminate state, unassured about salvation and eternal life. Timothy wrote in 2 Timothy 1:12 (NKJV): "for I <u>know</u> whom I have believed and am persuaded that He is able to keep what I have committed to Him until that Day." The key word being "know." And we know because we have His life in ours as seen in Galatians 2:20 (KJV) "the life which I now live in the flesh I live by the <u>faith of the Son of God.</u>"

As stated before, you cannot just "will" eternal life as was seen when Christ denied it to the rich young man although the rich young man wanted it. The granting of eternal life must come from the Father ("unless the Father who sent Me draws him" John 6:44 NKJV), which is called grace. "For by grace you have been saved through faith, and not of yourselves; it is the gift of God, not of works, lest anyone should boast." (Ephesians 2:8-9 NKJV) If it was "your will" to have salvation, God would be limited in His sovereignty, no longer in control of everything. You could also now take some credit for your salvation because "you decided to come to Christ," which would no longer now be complete grace but only partial grace. As you cannot will salvation, you also cannot "will" the assurance of eternal life, it has to come from the Father; it also comes by grace.

So what did Peter have that the rich young man did not have? Peter had the assurance of eternal life as well as a personal relationship with Christ. We need that as well. After Peter denied the Lord three times he must have felt very ashamed and uncomfortable. When Christ met Peter after His resurrection He asked Peter, "Do you love me?" Peter answered in John 21:16 (NKJV) saying, "Yes, Lord; You know that I love You." Peter was growing in the "good ground," continuing his relationship with Christ even though he had denied Christ in the past. You may say to yourself at this point, "I love the Lord and we have this love relationship, in fact I frequently go about my daily life singing praises to Him." But listen to how the Lord views this love relationship. "For whom the Lord loves He chastens, and scourges every son whom He receives. If you endure chastening, God deals with you as with sons; for what son is there whom a father does not chasten? But if you are without chastening, of which all have become partakers, then you are illegitimate and not sons." (Hebrews 12:6-8 NKJV) If you "endure chastening" and do not fall away like the seed by the wayside, in the rocky ground, or among the thorns, you will be treated as a son, growing in good ground.

This new relationship we have with God needs to have roots that go deep, so anything in our life that can be a detriment to this relationship must be exposed and "reckon yourselves to be dead indeed to sin, but alive to God in Christ Jesus our Lord" (Romans 6:11 NKJV), that "we also shall be in the likeness of His resurrection" (Romans 6:5 NKJV) and "walk in newness of life" (Romans 6:4 NKJV). This chastisement or unveiling of our natural life is necessary so we may be "conformed to the image of His Son" (Romans 8:29 NKJV) and "not be conformed to this world" (Romans 12:2 NKJV). We are told in 1 Corinthians 11:32 (NKJV): "But when we are judged we are chastened by the Lord, that we may not be condemned with the world." The Lord said to the Laodicean church in Revelation 3:19 (NKJV): "As many as I love, I rebuke and chasten. Therefore be zealous and repent." The answer to why all this chastening is found in Hebrews 12:10 (NKJV): "that they may be partakers of <u>His holiness.</u>" Christ's main desire for us. This whole discussion can be summed up by looking at the words written by Paul in Ephesians 1:4-5 (NKJV): "<u>He chose us in Him</u> before the foundation of the world, that <u>we should be holy and without blame before Him in love</u>, having predestined us to <u>adoption as sons by Jesus Christ</u> to Himself, according to the <u>good pleasure of His will</u>." Let me please add, not "our will."

So after a long period of being under the care of the Lord Jesus, Peter could write in 1 Peter 5:10 (NKJV): "But may the God of all <u>grace</u>, who <u>called</u> us to His <u>eternal glory</u> by Christ Jesus, after you have suffered a while, perfect, establish, strengthen and settle you." "Perfect, establish, strengthen and settle you" is what you call a secure relationship with Christ. Peter knew eternal life because the Holy Spirit made it real to him and he wants us to know we also can be made secure in our faith by telling us in 2 Peter 1:10 (NKJV) "to make your call and election sure."

Chapter 8
The Old and the New Man

Man, knowing good as well as evil, alienated himself from the life of God. Man, by his own effort, could try to please God to regain that relationship, but in God's eyes the good in our life cannot outweigh the evil. There needed to be some type of cleansing, a washing away or—better said—a death of the evil in our life. Watchman Nee had a good understanding what we inherited from Adam and Eve and how it was dealt with to bring back our relationship with God.

> We are all born "in Adam," and Romans 5:12-21 reveals to us what we are "in Adam." We are constituted sinners, not by the sins we commit, but by being in Adam. All of us sinned before we were born, because we were "in Adam" when he sinned. If your great-grandfather had died when he was three years old, where would you be? You would have died in him! Your experience was bound up with his. You are involved in Adam's sin, and by being born "in Adam" we receive all that is of Adam; that is, the Adam nature which is the nature of a sinner.
>
> The vital question then is, "How can I get out of Adam?" We came in by birth, therefore we can only get out by death and it is just this way of escape that God has provided. "All we who were baptized into Christ Jesus were baptized into his death" (Romans 6:3). To be "in Christ" is to have been identified with Him in His

death and resurrection. The Cross is the power of God which translates us from Adam into Christ.

In 1 Corinthians 15:45-47, the Lord Jesus Christ is called by two names—"the last Adam," and "the second Man." The Scripture does not refer to Him as the second Adam or as the last Man, for as the last Adam He is the sum total of humanity, and as the second Man He is the Head of a new race of man. As the last Adam He gathers up into Himself all that was in Adam; as the second Man, having by His Cross done away with the first man in whom God's purpose was frustrated, He brings in another Man in whom that purpose is fully realized. "Wherefore if any man is in Christ, there is a new creation; the old things are passed away; behold, they are become new" (2 Corinthians 5:17). By the Cross, God wiped out the whole of the old creation, and out of death a new creation is brought in, in Christ, the second Man. If we are "in Adam," all that is "in Adam" necessarily devolves upon us. Likewise, if we are "in Christ," all that is in Him comes to us by free grace without effort on our part, on the ground of simple faith.

(Twelve Baskets Full, Vol 3,
Watchman Nee)

In Adam all was lost. Through the disobedience of one man we were all constituted sinners. By him sin entered and death through sin, and throughout the race sin has reigned unto death from that day on. But now a ray of light is cast upon the scene. Through the obedience of Another we may be constituted righteous. Where sin abounded, grace did much more abound, and as sin reigned unto death, even so may grace reign through righteousness unto eternal life by Jesus Christ our Lord (Romans 5:19-21). Our despair is in Adam; our hope is in Christ.

God clearly intends that this consideration should lead to our practical deliverance from sin. Paul makes this quite plain when he opens chapter 6 of his letter with the question: "Shall we continue in sin?" His whole being recoils at the very suggestion. "God forbid!" he exclaims. How could a holy God be satisfied to have unholy, sin-fettered children? And so—"How shall we any longer live therein?" (Romans 6:1-2). God has surely therefore made adequate provision that we should be set free from sin's dominion.

But here is our problem: We were born sinners; how then can we cut off our sinful heredity? Seeing that we were born in Adam, how can we get out of Adam? Let me say at once, the Blood cannot take us out of Adam. There is only one way. Since we came in by birth we must go out by death. To do away with our sinfulness we must do away with our life. Bondage to sin came by birth; deliverance from sin comes by death—and it is just this way of escape that God has provided. Death is the secret of emancipation. "We died to sin" (Romans 6:2)

But how can we die? Some of us have tried very hard to get rid of this sinful life, but we have found it most tenacious. What is the way out? It is not by trying to kill ourselves, but by recognizing that God *has* dealt with us in Christ. This is summed up in the apostle's next statement: "All we who were baptized into Christ Jesus were baptized into His death" (Rom.6:3).

But if God has dealt with us "in Christ Jesus," then we have got to be in Him for this to become effective, and that now seems just as big a problem. How are we to "get into" Christ? Here again God comes to our help. We have in fact no way of getting in, but, what is more important, we need not *try* to get in, for we *are* in. What we could not do for ourselves, God has done for us. *He has put us* into Christ. Let me remind you of 1 Corinthians 1:30. I think that is one of the best verses of the whole New Testament: "Ye are in Christ." How? "Of Him (that is, "of God") are ye in Christ." Praise God! It is not left to us either to devise a way of entry or to work it out. We need not plan how to get in. God has planned it and He has not only planned it but He has also performed it. "Of Him are ye in Christ Jesus." We *are in*, therefore we need not *try* to get in. It is a divine act and it is accomplished.

> "Of Him are ye in Christ Jesus." The Lord God himself has put us in Christ, and in his dealing with Christ, God has dealt with the whole race. Our destiny is bound up with his. What he has gone through we have gone through, for to be "in Christ" is to have been identified with him in both his death and resurrection. He was crucified: then what about us? Must we ask God to crucify us? Never! When Christ was crucified we were crucified; and his crucifixion is past, therefore ours cannot be future. I challenge you to find one text in the New Testament telling us that our crucifixion is in the future. All the references to it are in the Greek aorist, which is the "once-for-all" tense, the "eternally past" tense. (See: Romans 6:6; Galatians 2:20; 5:24; 6:14) And just as no man could ever commit suicide by crucifixion, for it were a physical impossibility to do so, so also, in spiritual terms, God does not require us to crucify ourselves. We were crucified when Christ was crucified, for God put us there in him. That we have died in Christ is not merely a doctrinal position, it is an eternal and indisputable fact.
>
> (The Normal Christian Life, Watchman Nee)

Building on what Watchman Nee said concerning our co-death with Christ, let us now look at what coauthors Jamieson, Fausset and Brown have to say about our co-resurrection with Christ.

> The resurrection of Christ is here, as generally in the New Testament, ascribed to the Father, who therein proclaimed His judicial satisfaction with and acceptance of His whole work in the flesh, "even so we also should walk in newness of life." (Romans 6:4b KJV) The parallel here is not (as the apostle's language might seem to say) between Christ's resurrection and our *walking* in newness of life, but between Christ's resurrection and our *resurrection* to newness of life—henceforth to *walk* in it. Believers, immediately on their union to the risen Savior, rise to a new resurrection-life—the life, in fact, of their risen Lord—as is once and

> again emphatically expressed in the sequel. Here, taking this for granted, the apostle advances to the practical development of this new life, saying, in effect, 'That like as Christ was raised from the dead by the glory of the Father, even so we also, *risen with Him,* should, as new creatures, walk conformably.' But what is that "newness?" Surely if our *old life, now dead, and buried with Christ, was wholly* sinful, the *new,* to which we rise with the risen Savior, must be altogether a holy life; so that every time we go back to "those things whereof we are now ashamed" (Romans 6:21), we tell lies about our resurrection with Christ to newness of life, and "forget that we have been purged from our old sins" (2 Peter 1:9).
>
> (Bible Commentary Vol. 3, Jamieson, Fausset & Brown)

Realizing how this new state came about, we can see the holiness and freeness Christ offers. No longer a slave to our natural passions, we are now set free to serve Him in newness of life. Again Watchman Nee does well to explain this new relationship we have with God.

> Romans 6 deals with freedom from sin. Romans 7 deals with freedom from the Law. In chapter 6 Paul has told us how we could be delivered from sin, and we concluded that this was all that was required. Chapter 7 now teaches that deliverance from sin is not enough, but that we also need to know deliverance from the Law. If we are not fully emancipated from the Law, we can never know full emancipation from sin. But what is the difference between deliverance from sin and deliverance from the Law? We all see the value of the former, but where, we wonder, is the need for the latter? For the answer, we must first of all ask ourselves what the Law is, and what is its special value for us.
>
> Romans 7 has a new lesson to teach us. It is found in the discovery that I am "in the flesh" (Romans 7:5), that "I am carnal" (7:14), and that "in me, that is, in my flesh, dwelleth no good thing" (7:18). This goes beyond the question of sin, for it relates also to

the matter of pleasing God. We are dealing here not with sin in its forms but with, man in his carnal state. The latter includes the former, but it takes us a stage further, for it leads to the discovery that in this realm too we are totally impotent, and that "they that are in the flesh cannot please God" (Romans 8:8). How then is this discovery made? It is made with the help of the Law.

Let us retrace our steps for a minute and attempt to describe what is probably the experience of many. Many a Christian is truly saved and yet bound by sin. It is not that he is necessarily living under the power of sin all the time, but that there are certain particular sins hampering him continually so that he commits them over and over again. One day he hears the full message of the Gospel, that the Lord Jesus not only died to cleanse away our sins, but that when He died He included us sinners in His death; so that not only were our sins dealt with, but we ourselves were dealt with too. The man's eyes are opened and he knows he has been crucified with Christ. Two things follow that revelation. In the first place he reckons that he has died and risen with his Lord. In the second place, recognizing God's claim upon him, and that he has no more right over himself, he presents himself to God as alive from the dead. This is the commencement of a beautiful Christian life, full of praise to the Lord.

But then he begins to reason as follows: "I have died with Christ and am raised with Him, and I have given myself over to Him for ever; now I must do something for Him, since He has done so much for me. I want to please Him and do His will." So, after the step of consecration, he seeks to discover the will of God, and sets himself to carry it out. Then he makes a strange discovery. He thought he could do the will of God, because he thought he loved it, but gradually he finds he does not always like it at all. At times he even feels a distinct reluctance to pursue it, and often when he tries to put it into practice, he finds he cannot. Then he begins to question his experience. He asks himself: "Did I really know? Yes! Did I really reckon? Yes! Did I really give myself to him? Yes! Have I withdrawn my consecration? No! Then whatever is the matter now?" For the more this man tries to do the will of God the more he fails. Ultimately he comes to the conclusion that he never really loved God's will at all, so he prays for the desire as well as the power to do it. He confesses his disobedience and promises never to disobey again. But scarcely has he got up from his knees when he falls once more; before he reaches the point of victory, he is conscious of defeat. Then he says to himself: "Perhaps my last decision was not definite enough. This time I will be absolutely definite." So he brings all his willpower to bear on the situation, only to find greater defeat than ever awaiting him the next time a choice has to be made. Then at last he echoes the words of Paul: "For I know that in me, that is, in my flesh, dwelleth no good thing: for to will is present with me, but to do that which is good is not. For the good which I would I do not: but the evil which I would not, that I practice" (Romans 7:18, 19). He has reached the point of desperation.

Many Christians find themselves suddenly launched into the experience of Romans 7 and they do not understand why. They fancy Romans 6 is quite enough. Having grasped that, they think there can be no more question of failure, and then to their utmost surprise they find themselves right in the midst of Romans 7. What is the explanation?

First, let us be quite clear that the death with Christ described in Romans 6 is fully adequate to cover all our need. It is the explanation of that death, with all that follows from it in chapter 6, that is as yet incomplete. We are still in ignorance of the truth set forth in chapter 7. For Romans 7 is given to us to explain and make real the statement in Romans 6:14, that: "Sin shall not have dominion over you: for ye are not under law, but under grace." The trouble is that we do not yet know deliverance from law. What, then, is the meaning of Law?

Grace means that God does something for me; law means that I do something for God. God has certain holy and righteous demands which he places upon me: that is law. Now if law means that God requires something of me for their fulfillment, then deliverance from law means that he no longer requires that from me, but Himself provides it. Law implies that God requires me to do something for Him; deliverance from law implies that He exempts me from doing it, and that in grace he does it Himself. I (where "I" is the "carnal" man of chapter 7:14) need do nothing for God: that is deliverance from law. The trouble in Romans 7 is that man in the flesh tried to do something for God. As soon as you try to please God in that way, then you place yourself under law, and the experience of Romans 7 begins to be yours.

As we seek to understand this, let it be settled at the outset that the fault does not lie with the Law. Paul says, "the law is holy, and the commandment holy, and righteous, and good" (Romans 7:12). No, there is nothing wrong with the Law, but there is something decidedly wrong with me. The demands of the Law are righteous, but the person upon whom the demands are made is unrighteous. The trouble is not that the Law's demands are unjust, but that I am unable to meet them. It may be all right for the Government to require payment of 100 pounds, but it will be all wrong if I have only ten shillings with which to meet the payment!

I am a man "sold under sin" (Romans 7:14). Sin has dominion over me. True, as long as you leave me alone I seem to be rather a fine type of man. It is when you ask me to do something that my sinfulness comes to light.

If you have a very clumsy servant and he just sits still and does nothing, then his clumsiness does not appear. If he does nothing all day he will be of little use to you, it is true, but at least he will do no damage that way. But if you say to him: "Now come along, don't idle away your time: get up and do something," then immediately the trouble begins. He knocks the chair over as he gets up, stumbles over a footstool a few paces further on, then smashes some precious dish as soon as he handles it. If you make no demands upon him his clumsiness is never noticed, but as soon as you ask him to do anything his awkwardness is apparent at once. The demands were all right, but the man was all wrong. He was as clumsy a man when he was sitting still as when he was working, but it was your demands that made manifest the clumsiness which, whether he was active or inactive, was all the time in his make-up.

We are all sinners by nature. If God asks nothing of us, all seems to go well, but as soon as He demands something of us, the occasion is provided for a grand display of our sinfulness. The Law makes our weakness manifest. While you let me sit still I appear to be all right, but when you ask me to do anything I am sure to spoil it, and if you trust me with a second thing I will as surely spoil that also. When a holy law is applied to a sinful man, then it is that his sinfulness comes out in full display.

God knows who I am; He knows that from head to foot I am full of sin; He knows that I am weakness incarnate; that I can do nothing. The trouble is that I do not know it. I admit that all men are sinners, and that therefore I am a sinner; but I imagine that I am not such a hopeless sinner as some. God must bring us all to the place where we see that we are utterly weak and helpless. While we say so, we do not wholly believe it, and God has to do something to convince us of the fact. Had it not been for the Law, we should never have known how weak we are. Paul had reached that point. He makes this clear when he says in Romans 7:7: "I had not known sin, except through the law: for I had not known coveting, except the law had said, thou shalt not covet." Whatever might be his experience with the rest of the Law, it was the tenth commandment, which literally translated is, "Thou shalt not desire..." that found him out. There his total incapacity stared him in the face!

The more we try to keep the Law the more our weakness is manifest and the deeper we get into Romans 7, until it is clearly demonstrated to us that we are hopelessly weak. God knew it all along, but we did not, and so God had to bring us through painful experiences to a recognition of the fact. We need to have our weakness proved to ourselves beyond dispute. That is why God gave us the Law.

So we can say, reverently, that God never gave us the Law to keep: He gave us the Law to break! He well knew that we could not keep it. We are so bad that He asks no favor and makes no demands. Never has any man succeeded in making himself acceptable to God by means of the Law. Nowhere in the New Testament are men of faith told that they are to keep the Law; but it does say that the Law was given so that there should be transgression. "The law came in... that the trespass might abound" (Romans 5:20). The Law was given to make us law-breakers! No doubt I am a sinner in Adam; "Howbeit, I had not known sin, except through the law:... for apart from the law sin is dead... but when the commandment came, sin revived, and I died" (Romans 7:7-9). The Law is that which exposes our true nature. Alas, we are so conceited, and think ourselves so strong, that God has to give us something to test us and prove how weak we are. At last we see it, and confess, "I am a sinner through and through, and of my self I can do nothing whatever to please holy God."

No, the Law was not given in the expectation that we would keep it. It was given in the full knowledge that we would break it; and when we have broken it so completely as to be convinced of our utter need, then the Law has served its purpose. It has been our schoolmaster to bring us to Christ, that in us He may himself fulfill it (Galatians 3:24).

(The Normal Christian Life,
Watchman Nee)

Chapter 9
Faith

Webster's dictionary defines faith as a "firm belief in something for which there is no proof." The Bible has much to say about faith and its substance. Man's interpretation of God's Holy Word has occasionally muddied the waters of understanding, and a careful look at "Faith" in the Bible reveals insight about the character of God and of man.

Through the years, Bible translators attempt to make the Bible more readable and in so doing have changed the true meaning of some portions of scripture. For instance, in Galatians 2:20 the preposition "of" in the King James Version has been replaced with the preposition "in" in other versions. The KJV says: "the life which I now live in the flesh I live by the faith of the Son of God" while the New King James Version (NKJV) says: "the life which I now live in the flesh I live by faith in the Son of God." This small change puts faith on a slippery slope. A faith in God can falter because it is the faith of man toward God, where the faith of God will stand firm no matter the trial set before it. This is not the only instance where the preposition "of" has been replaced with the preposition "in." Below are some other examples where the word "of" is used in the KJV and replaced by the word "in" for other translations.

> Ephesians 3:12 KJV: "In whom we have boldness and access with confidence by the faith _of_ him."

Philippians 3:9-10 KJV: "And be found in him, not having my own righteous, which is of the law, but that which is through the faith <u>of</u> Christ, the righteousness which is of God by faith; that I may know him, and the power of his resurrection, and the fellowship of his sufferings, being made conformable unto his death."

1 Corinthians 2:5 KJV: "That your faith should not stand in the wisdom of men, but in the power <u>of</u> God."

Romans 4:16 KJV: "Therefore, it is <u>of</u> faith, that it might be by grace."

Galatians 2:16 KJV: "Knowing that a man is not justified by the works of the law, but by the faith <u>of</u> Jesus Christ."

Galatians 3:22 KJV: "But the scriptures hath concluded all under sin, that the promise by faith <u>of</u> Jesus Christ might be given to them that believe."

To uncover the real meaning of these passages and better understand what the God-inspired authors of the Bible were trying to say, let us begin by understanding how this whole process of us becoming a Christian began. A. W. Pink, in his exposition on Hebrews, details God's initiative in salvation and emphasizes the faith of God in the passages below.

> The salvation of God does not actually become ours until we believe in, rest upon, and receive Christ as a personal Savior. But we cannot see without both sight and light, neither can we believe until life and faith are divinely communicated to us. "For by grace are ye saved through faith; and that not of yourselves: it is the gift of God: not of works, lest any man should boast" (Ephesians 2:8-9 KJV). As God must give me breath before I can breathe, so faith ere I believe. Compare also "faith which is by him" (Acts 3:16 KJV); "who believe, according to the working of his mighty

power" (Ephesians 1:19 KJV); "through the faith of the operation of God" (Colossians 2:12 KJV); "who by him do believe in God" (1 Peter 1:21 KJV).

While it is the bound duty of every sinner to repent (Acts 17:30)—for ought he not to cease from and abhor his rebellion against God?—yet he is so completely under the blinding power of sin that a miracle of grace is necessary before he will do so. A broken and a contrite spirit are of God's providing. It is the Holy Spirit who illuminates the understanding to perceive the heinousness of sin, the heart to loathe it, and the will to repudiate it. Faith and repentance are the first evidence of spiritual life. For when God quickens a sinner He convicts him of the evil of sin, causes him to hate it, moves him to sorrow over and turn from it. "Surely after I was turned *away*, I repented; and after I was instructed, I smote upon *my* thigh; I was ashamed, yea, even confounded" (Jeremiah 31:19 KJV). "if God perhaps will give them repentance" (2 Timothy 2:25 KJV).

To be saved by grace and not of ourselves (Ephesians 2:8-9), God must have given us the faith to believe. And as one person has said; "it took two of us for me to come to Christ, Christ to draw me to Him and for me to fight against Him every step of the way."

Let us look at the Christian in his journey after salvation. The Hebrew Christians in Hebrew 6:6 were trying to "crucify to themselves the Son of God afresh." They did not realize the sufficiency of the finished work of Christ and were toiling to regain their position rather than resting in the provisions He had provided which included faith. The author of Hebrews says in Hebrews 6:1 (KJV) "Therefore, leaving the principles of the doctrine of Christ, let us go on unto perfection, not laying again the foundation of repentance from dead works, and of faith toward God." Rather than having a faith toward God, they needed to recognize they now had the faith "of" God. "Christ's sacrifice has expiated our sins, when the spirit applies its virtues to the heart, that is, when He gives faith to appropriate them, our sense of guilt is removed, peace is communicated, and we are enabled to approach God not only without dread, but as joyous worshippers." (Exposition of Hebrews, A. W. Pink)

We now live under this new covenant stated in Hebrews 8:10 (KJV): "I will put my laws into their mind, and write them in their hearts; and I will be to them a God, and they shall be to me a people." Also a rest for believers is spoken of in Hebrews 4:9-10 (KJV): "There remaineth, therefore, a rest to the people of God. For he that is entered into his rest, he also hath ceased from his own works, as God did from his." Ceasing from our own works, our own faith and resting in the fact He is our life, our faith, our joy, our peace. We now have the faith "of" God spoken of as fruit in Galatians 5:22; let us rest in that fact. The fruits were given to us as believers when we became saved and received the Holy Spirt.

How can we be "conformed to the image of his Son" (Romans 8:29 KJV) if there is anything in us of ourselves. We are conformed to the image of His Son when we have His faith in us, His love in us, His joy in us. So what if a Christian concludes that the correct reading should be the faith "of" God but that fact is not a reality in his life. I will again quote A. W. Pink, from a passage of his book "The Nature of God", where he will give some insight into this problem.

> The unawakened are unconcerned about the glory of God and indifferent as to whether their conduct pleases Him. They have no concept of the sinfulness of sin and no realization of how completely sin dominates them. Only when the Spirit of God illumines their minds and convicts their consciences do they see the awfulness of their state; and only then, as they try to reform their ways, are they conscious of the might of their inward foe and of their inability to cope with him. In vain deliverance is sought in resolutions and endeavors in our own strength. Even after we are quickened and begin to understand the Gospel, for a season (often a lengthy one) it is rather a fight than a rest. But as we grow more out of ourselves and are taught to live in Christ and draw our strength from Him by faith, we obtain a rest in this respect also.

56 God's Purpose

As the believer realizes more clearly the sufficiency of the finished work of Christ, he is delivered experientially from the Law and sees that he no longer owes it service. His obedience is no longer legal but evangelical, no longer out of fear, but out of, gratitude. His service to the Lord is not in a servile, but in a gracious spirit. What was formerly a burden is now a delight. He no longer seeks to earn God's favor, but acts in the realization that the smile of God is upon him. Far from rendering him careless, this will spur him on to strive to glorify the One who gave His own Son as a sacrifice. Thus, bondage gives place to liberty; slavery, to sonship; toil, to rest. And the soul reposes on the unchangeable Word of Christ and follows Him steadily through light and darkness.

Try as we might, you may not feel you have liberty and rest but only struggle and doubt. But before you get too discouraged, read this story of one of the great missionaries of the Christian era, Hudson Taylor. Born in England in 1832, he accepted Christ when he was 17 years old, studied medicine, was led of the Lord to be a missionary to the interior of China, and founded the China Inland Mission. After all this, you would think he was the model Christian, but a letter written to his mother at 37 years old reveals something different.

> My own position becomes continually more and more responsible, and my need greater of special grace to fill it; but I have continually to mourn that I follow at such a distance and learn so slowly to imitate my precious Master. I cannot tell you how I am buffeted sometimes by temptation. I never knew how bad a heart I had.
> Yet I do know that I love God and love His work, and desire to serve Him only and in all things. And I value above all things that precious Savior in whom alone I can be accepted. Often I am tempted to think that one so full of sin cannot be a child of God at all; but I try to throw it back, and rejoice all the more in the preciousness of Jesus, and the riches of that grace that has made

us "accepted in the Beloved." Beloved He is of God; beloved He ought to be of us. But oh, how short I fall here again!

May God help me to love Him more and serve Him better. Do pray for me. Pray that the Lord will keep me from sin, will sanctify me wholly, will use me more largely in His service.

From the previous letter written to his mother and the following letter written to his sister something happened that changed his life. As you read it try to see what was revealed to Hudson Taylor.

As to work, mine was never so plentiful, so responsible, or so difficult; but the weight and strain are all gone. The last month or more has been perhaps, the happiest of my life; and I long to tell you a little of what the Lord has done for my soul. I do not know how far I may be able to make myself intelligible about it, for there is nothing new or strange or wonderful—and yet, all is new! In a word, "Whereas once I was blind, now I see...."

When my agony of soul was at its height, a sentence in a letter from dear McCarthy was to remove the scales from my eyes, and the Spirit of God revealed the truth of our oneness with Jesus as I had never known it before. McCarthy, who had been much excised by the same sense of failure, but saw the light before I did, wrote (I quote from memory): "But how to get faith strengthened? Not by striving after faith, but by resting on the Faithful One."

As I read I saw it all! "If we believe not, He abideth faithful." I looked to Jesus and saw (and when I saw, oh, how joy flowed!) that He had said, "I will never leave you." "Ah, there is rest!" I thought. "I have striven in vain to rest in Him. I'll strive no more. For has He not promised to abide with me— never to leave me, never to fail me?" And, dearie, He never will!

But this was not all He showed me, nor one half. As I thought of the vine and the branches, what light the blessed Spirit poured into my soul! How great seemed my mistake in having wished to get the sap, the fullness out of Him. I saw not only that Jesus

> would never leave me, but that I was a member of His body, of His flesh and of His bones. The vine, now I see is not the root merely, but all—root, stem, branches, twigs, leaves, flowers, fruit: and Jesus is not only that: He is soil and sunshine, air and showers, and ten thousand times more than we have ever dreamed, wished for, or needed. Oh, the joy of seeing this truth! I do pray that the eyes of your understanding may be enlightened, that you may know and enjoy the riches freely given us in Christ.
>
> The sweetest part, if one may speak of one part being sweeter than another, is the rest which full identification with Christ brings. I am no longer anxious about anything, as I realize this; for He, I know, is able to carry out His will, and His will is mine. It makes no matter where He places me, or how. That is rather for Him to consider than for me; for in the easiest positions He must give me His grace, and in the most difficult His grace is sufficient.

Hudson Taylor went from a faith "in" God to the faith "of" God. What seems natural to us as we continue in our Christian journey is that we think we should be growing in faith, and there is at least one verse to support this theory. 2 Thessalonians 1:3 (KJV) says; "We are bound to thank God always for you, brethren, as it is fitting, because your faith groweth exceedingly, and the love of every one of you all toward each other aboundeth." But if our faith is "of" God, how is it possible to grow? 2 Peter 3:18 (KJV) tells us to "grow in grace, and in the knowledge of our Lord and Savior, Jesus Christ." By growing in grace and knowledge your realization of what we have in Him becomes more apparent. There is no more striving or praying for more faith, but resting in His faith. Growing in faith happens like this: First, a spark is ignited in our life of who God is, then as time goes on, we see how He lives and works in our lives, and finally we see He is our all and all, His life in ours, His faith in us. A. B. Simpson in "The Christ in the Bible Commentary" speaks of this kind of faith.

> For our faith is just as much the work of Christ as our holiness, our love or any of the graces of Christian life. When He comes to

abide within us He simply imparts to us His own nature and Spirit, and puts into our heart the very same sentiments of trust toward His Father which He Himself ever cherished. There is nothing so delightful as this consciousness of the very life and heart of Christ within us, the trust that springs spontaneously within our breast, the prayer that prays itself, and the song that sings in joyous triumph even when all around is dark and strange.

So let us not be like those who came out of Egypt and did not enter the Canaan rest because of <u>unbelief</u> (Hebrews 3:19). They did not have the faith "of" God as Joshua and Caleb did. But "Let us, therefore, fear lest, a promise being left us of entering into his rest, any of you should seem to come short of it." (Hebrews 4:1 KJV) Continuing with Hebrews 10:38 (KJV) we are told "the just shall live by faith; but if any man draw back, my soul shall have no pleasure in him." And, "Therefore we also, since we are surrounded by so great a cloud of witness, let us lay aside every weight, and the sin which so easily ensnares us, and let us run with endurance the race that is set before us, looking unto Jesus, the author and finisher of our faith" (Hebrews 12:1-2a NKJV).

One more point. Hebrews 11:3 KJV says: "Through faith we understand that the worlds were framed by the word of God, so that things which are seen were not made of things which do appear." We know the world was created by God because His faith makes us know against all the theories of man on how it does appear to be made. A faith that makes us know who made the world, a faith that knows we are saved and going to heaven, a faith that knows "that our old man was crucified with Him" (Romans 6:6 NKJV) and "Now if we died with Christ, we believe that we shall also live with Him" (Romans 6:8 NKJV). Live with Him now, not only in eternity.

Chapter 10
Suffering

There is a need for us to understand what God's purpose is for suffering and no better example to use than Job of the Old Testament.

The book of Job reveals to us the place and purpose of suffering in the spiritual life. In the history of Job we are shown, subjectively, the stage of growth when suffering becomes *a necessary part of God's training* in conforming His children to the "pattern" Son, who is the Firstborn among many brethren.

In the history of Job the earlier stages of the Christian life are not depicted at all; the story *begins at the point where many place the goal.*

Job, so said Jehovah, was in His sight blameless (not faultless), true, Godly and eschewing evil! What better description could we have of the life of victory over sin, of surrender to the will of God, and of obedience to the known commands of God? What better description of a life in the power of the Holy Spirit than that which fell from Job's own lips, recorded in Job chapter 29?

The story of Job's life therefore teaches us that the "life of God in the soul of man" must come to some *maturity of growth* before the child of God is ready for the lessons of the crucible, where he will learn to "endure unto chastening" and be dealt with as a son in whom the Father delighteth (Proverbs 3:12), and whom He scourgeth (Hebrews 12:6-10) that he may be a partaker of His holiness.

Job was an object lesson for the people of God throughout all time, therefore every aspect of trial was allowed to come upon him. With other of His children, the Lord will perhaps use but one of Job's many sorrows to bring them to the same place of blessing.

To some may come the loss of all earthly substance; to others the removal of loved ones to the heavenly home; and yet to others the stripping of strength and the lesson of helpless weakness. The All-wise Father knows each child of His love, the peculiar temperament and character, the particular danger and need; and so He lovingly adapts His training to the individual soul.

Some naturally love an active life, and need to be taught to lie still; others shrink from activity and would gladly live in quiet retreat. These latter He may choose to face the glare and pain of aggressive service, while the ones who love the bustle and noise are bidden, "Go, shut thyself within thy house." Others, again, are full of energy and strength, and only learn with bitter tears how to keep step with God, while slothful, easy-going souls are taught to find their *energy* in Him!

In any case, the Scriptures plainly teach us that, in many and varied ways, the ripest servants of God are *led through the same pathway of trial*. The "object lessons" are repeated, so that we may not fail to understand the ways of the Lord.

If we compare the language of David in Psalm 69 with chapter 30 of the book of Job, we see how both were led through the same deep waters in very different circumstances.

Again, if we compare Lamentations 3 with the same chapter in the book of Job, we find the words of Jeremiah and Job to be almost alike in the outpouring of grief in their hour of affliction.

Yet once more, we find a similar cry of the soul in the language, of Jonah when in the belly of the "sea monster"—in this case specifically said by the Lord Himself to represent His own passage through Calvary and the grave to the right hand of the Majesty on high.

The scene in heaven conclusively shows that one object of Job's trial was to prove to the heavenly principalities and powers the "*manifold wisdom of God*" (Ephesians 3:10), for, as the heavenly hosts looked on at the tested servant of God upon earth, they saw the wisdom of God in His masterly way of changing the satanic attempt to ruin Job into a means of greater and richer blessing to his soul.

The Lord *proved to the angels* that His plan of bringing men through death to life was worthy of His infinite wisdom and His knowledge of the character of man. He proved, also, to the heavenly powers that He is able to obtain disinterested (free from self-interest) love and service from His servants on earth.

The Lord *proved to the devil* that Job did not serve Jehovah for all the blessings he had received from Him, and that all attacks upon the children of God only lead them closer to their Lord, so long as they trust the faithfulness of God and do not withdraw themselves from His hand.

The Lord *proved to Job* that the END of all His dealings with His children is for their eternal good, and that His character of love and pity is not changed when He places His servant in the crucible. Job himself acknowledged that Jehovah's dealings with him had been right, as in the searchlight of His presence he looked back upon his past, remembered his self-vindication, and loathed himself.

The Lord *proved to the friends* that a man could be justified before the Lord and walk with Him in integrity of heart, and that suffering is not invariably the result of transgression.

The Lord *proves to the children* of God through all the ages that they need the lessons of the crucible to make them know themselves, and, still more, a direct interview with Him before they truly can renounce themselves and know the abundant life in union with the risen Lord.

The glimpse into the heavenly court gives us not only knowledge of Jehovah's complete control over the Adversary but some knowledge of the devil's character and attitude towards the servants of God.

We are shown (and this is of vital importance to us today, over three thousand years since the story of Job was written) that the devil sets his heart upon every child of God who seeks to shun evil and to walk before the Lord with singleness of purpose and loyal integrity, and that he does not cease to use every subtle means to break their fellowship with God. Yet let us remember:

"I give unto them eternal life; and they shall never perish, and no one shall snatch them out of My hand," said the Lord Jesus to His disciples, adding, "My Father is greater than all; and no one is able to snatch them out of the Father's hand. I and the Father are one" (John 10:28-30).

The story of Job reveals the strength of the tie of life between the Lord and His children. The adversary is allowed to bring to bear upon it every possible test, yet it stands them all!

Property gone—but Job's treasures are in heaven! Children gone—but he had committed them to God and offered sacrifice for them, and they were safe in the Lord's keeping! Job himself, stricken and broken on every side, longs for death and cries to God to let him alone, but even in his anguish he refuses to part with the anchor of his soul! He persists that he is *in the hand of God*; and by his faith that he *was there*, he *abode* therein!

Let the redeemed take heed that they "keep [themselves] in the love of God" (see Jude 21 and John 15:9-10) and by faith abide under His mighty hand, so that He may exalt them in due time. Let them remember that the devil can touch them only so far as he is given permission by the Lord, but also only so far as *they give him permission too*!

The Lord may have permitted him to attack you on every side, but take heed that you give him *no further license than the Lord has allowed him* by listening to his whispered words that your God has forsaken you. "Hope thou in God and thou shalt yet praise Him, who is the health of thy countenance, and thy God."

Cruden says that "hand," when referring to God, signifies (1) *His eternal purposes* and *executive power*; (2) *His corrections*; (3) *His sovereign disposal*; (4) *His providence*, etc., etc.

Job, in saying that the "hand of God" had touched him, meant simply that the sovereign will of God had decreed his afflictions.

Satan was obliged to acknowledge the sovereignty of God when he said to Jehovah, "*Put forth Thine hand now*, and touch all that he hath" and again, "*Put forth Thine hand now*, and touch his bone and his flesh."

Jehovah replied, "Behold, all that he hath is in thy power"— thus by His sovereign will permitting the attack of the enemy, while by His divine control He made it *actually* true that Job and his times were yet in *His hand*.

In Ezekiel 22:17-22 the Lord tells Ezekiel that He will deal with Israel as men deal with precious metals. "As they gather silver and brass and iron and lead and tin into the midst of the furnace, to blow the fire upon it, to melt it... as silver is melted in the midst of the furnace, so shall ye be melted in the midst thereof." For the house of Israel had become dross to the Lord, and the fire that was to melt them was the fire of His wrath in terrible judgments.

It may be said that a soul walking with God as Job did could not be subject to the same "fire" as Ezekiel described to Israel; but the Apostle Paul speaks of a "judging" of the children of God that is inevitable.

The "judgment" that is coming upon the world must begin with the house of God, that the children of the family of God be not "*condemned with the world*" (1 Peter 4:17, 1 Corinthians 11:32).

The "dross" in Israel and the dross in the character of the faithful servant of God are alike abhorrent to the Lord, and alike are to be dealt with by His fire.

It may also be said that the Lord Himself is the refiner's fire to His separated ones: "Our God is a consuming fire." But again it is written by Isaiah that He purges by "*the spirit of judgment*, and by the spirit of burning," so that both are true.

The All-wise Lord turns His hand upon His children to thoroughly purge away their dross (Isaiah 1:25) even while He Himself is like a refiner's fire in the midst of them, for it is written that He shall "*sit as a refiner* and purifier of silver, and He shall purify the sons of Levi [His separated ones] and purge them as gold and silver." Also, our glorified Lord, the Faithful Witness, speaks yet again as He did to the Laodicean church (typical of these last days), and counsels us to "buy" (or obtain from Him at all costs) the "*gold refined by fire*" that we may "become rich" and, clothed with "white garments"—white with the white-heat of the furnace He has brought us through—be ready for His appearing.

"And some of them that be wise shall fall [or *be feeble*, as the word in the original means], to *refine* them [refers to the expulsion of dross by the smelting fire], and to *purify* [refers to the separation or removal of the dross already expelled] and to *make them white* [refers to the polishing and brightening of the metal after it has been freed from its impurity], even to the time of the end" (Daniel 11:35). (G. H. Pember, Great Prophesies of the Century)

(The Story of Job (Appendix),
Jessie Penn-Lewis)

After receiving Christ, we now have residing in us an altogether new nature which was not there before. In this human life we still do retain within us the old carnal (or flesh, or self, or Adam) nature, which now battles against this new spiritual nature. In order for us to be spirit controlled rather than flesh controlled, the Lord needs to do a refining by "fire" in our life. The dross (natural life) needs to be separated from the pure metal (spiritual life). This new holy life has divine power (by the Holy Spirit), if allowed, to overcome all of the temptations of this world that formerly plagued us, which we could not overcome in our own strength. God does not try to change or refine the old nature with which we were born as our inheritance from our father Adam. No, He has provided a "death" on Christ's cross for that self-nature when we are willing to accept it. Not only a death with Him but we also are raised with Him to walk in newness of life (Romans 6:2-13).

God's Purpose

Then He tells us: "If then you were raised with Christ, seek those things which are above, where Christ is sitting at the right hand of God. Set your mind on things above, not on things of the earth, for you died, and your life is hid with Christ in God" (Colossians 3:1-3 KJV). Then, by Christ's resurrection power learning daily to "walk by faith, not by sight" (2 Corinthians 5:7 KJV). So when suffering comes into our life, we must fully rely on Him and exercise this new life we have been given. God's object in having us to suffer is to bring us into conformity to His Son, who suffered for us.

> God "worketh all things after the counsel of his own will" (Ephesians 1:11 KJV)—the Greek for "worketh" means "to work effectually." For this reason we read, "For of him, and through him, and to him, are all things: to whom be glory forever. Amen" (Romans 11:36 KJV). Men may boast they are free agents, with a will of their own, and are at liberty to do as they please. But Scripture says to those who boast, "We will go into such a city, and continue there a year, and buy and sell," that they ought to say, "If the Lord will" (James 4:13, 15 KJV).
>
> Here then is a sure resting place for the heart. Our lives are neither the product of blind fate nor the result of capricious chance. Every detail of them was ordained from all eternity and is now ordered by the living, reigning God. Not a hair of our heads can be touched without His permission. "A man's heart deviseth his way: but the LORD directeth his steps" (Proverbs 16:9 KJV). What assurance, what strength, what comfort this should give the real Christian! "My times are in thy hand" (Psalm 31:15 KJV). Then let me "rest in the LORD, and wait patiently for him" (Psalm 37:7 KJV).
>
> (Gleanings In The Godhead,
A. W. Pink)

Job went through horrific trials, not by accident, but as God deemed them necessary. We also will go through difficult trials but let us have the attitude the Lord commanded Job to have, "Brace yourself like a man" (Job 40:7 NIV).

Chapter 11
Destiny

Satan

That God will yet permit the Devil to bring forth the satanic Masterpiece, who shall defy God and persecute His people, should scarcely be surprising. In each succeeding age there has been a Cain for every Abel; a Jannes and Jambres for every Moses and Aaron; a Babylon for every Jerusalem; an Herod for every John the Baptist. It has been so during this dispensation: the sowing of the Wheat was followed by the sowing of the Tares. It will be so in the Tribulation period; not only will there be a faithful remnant of Israel, but there shall be an unfaithful company of that people too. And just before the Christ of God returns to this earth to set up His kingdom, God will suffer His arch-enemy to bring forth the false christ, who will establish his kingdom.

(The Antichrist,
A. W. Pink)

At the end of this age there will be a period of cataclysmic events called "The Great Tribulation." During this period the Antichrist will try to mimic Christ and set up the Devil's kingdom here on earth. When Christ returns to earth the second time at the end of the seven year tribulation period He will defeat the armies of the beast (Antichrist) and the false prophet (Antispirit) and an angel will lay "hold of the dragon, that serpent of old, who is the Devil and Satan, and bind him for a thousand years" (Revelation 20:2 NKJV). Here we see the Trinity of Evil. There will be a 1000 year period after the tribulation where Christ shall rule on earth. At the end of this period of time, the devil will be loosed for a short period to again continue his work of drawing people away from God only to be cut short and finally, "The devil, who deceived them, was cast into the lake of fire and brimstone where the beast and the false prophet are. And they will be tormented day and night forever and ever" (Revelation 20:10 NKJV).

Unredeemed Man

Our sufferings will only be for a relatively short period of time while on earth whereas the unbeliever will suffer forever, "and anyone not found written in the Book of Life was cast into the lake of fire" (Revelation 20:15 NKJV).

Redeemed Man

When the Lord returns we shall be changed—our spirit, soul and body will change from corruption to incorruption, and from mortality to immortality. No longer will we fear death, for death will be swallowed up in victory! And we shall go to live with Him through all Eternity!

Christ

Christ is indeed the anointed of the Lord, the Author and Finisher of our faith, Emmanuel (God with us), the Holy One of God, and King Eternal; yet He died for, and lives for His people, His redeemed, of whom He is the Head. The Father, Son and the Holy Spirit are one and the same God, yet the Father has designated certain tasks for His Son and the Holy Spirit to carry out, especially to redeem His people on earth. As you read Revelation, the last book of the Bible you will see the completion of that goal. The redeemed in the book of life will spend eternity with Him and all the evil forces will be contained in hell to be locked away forever. Jesus and the Holy Spirit's mission have been completed. When Christ has "put down all rule and all authority and power" (1 Corinthians 15:24 KJV) and destroyed the last enemy, death (1 Corinthians 15:26), "then the Son Himself will also be subject to Him who put all things under Him, that God may be all in all" (1 Corinthians 15:28 NKJV). Each of the three were always God but in different forms to carry out His plan. Now the Son and the Holy Spirit can become One as in the beginning, so "that God may be all and in all." Mission accomplished as seen in John 17:1-11 (NKJV):

> Jesus spoke these words, lifted up His eyes to heaven, and said: "Father, the hour has come. Glorify Your Son, that Your Son also may glorify You, as You have given Him authority over all flesh, that He should give eternal life to as many as You have given Him. And this is eternal life, that they may know You, the only true God, and Jesus Christ whom You have sent. I have glorified You on the earth. I have finished the work which You have given Me to do. And now, O Father, glorify Me together with Yourself, with the <u>glory which I had with You before the world was</u>. I have manifested Your name to men whom You have given Me out of the world. They were Yours, You have gave them to Me, and they have kept Your word. Now they have known that all things which You have given Me are from You. For I have given to them the words which You have given Me; and they have received them, and have known surely that I came forth from You; and they have believed that You sent Me. I pray for them. I do not pray for the world but for those whom You have given Me, for they are Yours. And all Mine are Yours, and Yours Mine, and I am glorified in them. Now I am no longer in the world, but these are in the world, and I come to you. Holy Father, keep through Your name those whom You have given Me, <u>that they may be one as We are</u>."

Chapter 12
The Heart

Simply put, the heart is the inner source that governs outward performance. The mind makes decisions, but it is heavily influenced by the heart. To move from God's wrath to His mercy, something must be done about our sin nature. By looking at David as a primary example, we see the thread of God's grace woven through the Bible as He illuminates the problem of our sinful hearts, and comes to redeem us in our broken state. Once redeemed, we can then live in God's will and trust Him in the various circumstances of life.

> Inheriting a sin nature included receiving an evil heart as seen in Mark 7:21-22 (NKJV):
> For from within, out of the heart of men, proceed evil thoughts, adulteries, fornications, murders, thefts, covetousness, wickedness, deceit, lewdness, an evil eye, blasphemy, pride, foolishness.

So even though our heart may have many well-meaning desires and affections, it is overshadowed by a sin nature. "I the Lord, search the heart, I test the mind" (Jeremiah 17:10 NKJV). If the evil heart as described above governs our outward performance, how could we possibly do anything to please the One that searches and tests the heart? It would be hypocritical on our part to think that God would accept us in this horrific state. Jeremiah 17:9 (NKJV) says; "The heart is deceitful above all things, and desperately wicked; who can know it?" So, men and women are alienated from living a righteous life, "for all have sinned and fall short of the glory of God"

(Romans 3:23 NKJV), and alienated from God because their evil heart is the source that governs their motives. "Now, this is the position that God wants to bring us to, where we shall cease our struggles and our attempts at self-defense or self-improvement, and throw ourselves helplessly upon the mercy of God" (The Christ in the Bible Commentary, A. B. Simpson).

David knew self-improvement or sacrificing to God for the sins he committed fell short of pleasing Him. Not able to meet God's standards and knowing God needed to change him, David pours out his heart to God in Psalm 51:

> Have mercy upon me, O God,
> According to Your lovingkindness;
> According to the multitude of Your tender mercies,
> Blot out my transgressions.
> Wash me thoroughly from my iniquity,
> And cleanse me from my sin.
> For I acknowledge my transgressions,
> And my sin is always before me.
> Against You, You only, have I sinned,
> And done this evil in Your sight—
> That You may be found just when You speak,
> And blameless when You judge.
> Behold, I was brought forth in iniquity,
> And in sin my mother conceived me.
> Behold, You desire truth in the inward parts,
> And in the hidden part You will make me to know wisdom.
> Purge me with hyssop, and I shall be clean;
> Wash me, and I shall be whiter than snow.
> Make me hear joy and gladness,
> That the bones You have broken may rejoice.
> Hide Your face from my sins, and blot out all my iniquities.
> Create in me a clean heart, O God, and renew a steadfast spirit within me.
>
> Psalm 51:1-10 (NKJV)

> For You so not desire sacrifice, or else I would give it:
> You do not delight in burnt offering.
> The sacrifice of God are a broken spirit,
> A broken and contrite heart—
> These, O God, You will not despise.
>
> Psalm 51:16-17 (NKJV)

David knew "in sin my mother conceived me" and in order to have a proper relationship with God his natural life needed to be dealt with. He asked the Lord to purge and wash him and he "shall be whiter than snow." David knowing his helplessness to please God with his natural life offers his broken spirit and broken and contrite heart. God's response to what He thought of David can be seen in Acts 13:22 (NKJV).

> I have found David the son of Jesse, a man after My own heart, who will do all My will.

Notice how the right heart and doing God's will go hand in hand. David found grace in the eyes of God and that would carry him throughout life. Let us examine the twenty third Psalm which David wrote, to learn more of his life and thoughts.

> The Lord is my shepherd; I shall not want.
> He makes me to lie down in green pastures;
> He leads me beside the still waters.
>
> Psalm 23:1-2 (NKJV)

David speaks of the relationship he had between him and his creator and called Him "my shepherd". No matter what trials and temptations David went through he knew his Shepherd was there for him and was deeply concerned about him. David says his Shepard, "makes me to lie down" and leads me "besides still waters." David had an inner sense of security, a freedom from fear or worry.

God said of many in Israel that "They have forsaken Me, the fountain of living waters, and hewn themselves cisterns—broken cisterns that can hold no water (Jeremiah 2:13 NKJV). In other words, many have put other things in life before Him and attempt to worship God by their own self-effort and self-interest. Their hewn cistern, the one they built, were broken and could not hold the living water. David's cistern was hewn by God and held the living water, that still water that refreshes and satisfies. David then continues in Psalm 23:3:

> He restores my soul;
> He leads me in paths of righteousness
> For His name's sake.
>
> Psalm 23:3 (NKJV)

David realized his path in life was for "His name's sake", not for his own sake and enjoyment. We know this same thing from Ephesians 1:11 (NKJV): "according to the purpose of Him who works all things according to the counsel of His will" and His will being His good pleasure as seen in Isaiah 46:10 (NKJV): "My counsel shall stand, and I will do all My pleasure." When David was on a difficult path he poured his heart out to God and then moved on, not knowing what lay before him as seen in the next verse.

> Yea, though I walk through the valley of the shadow of death,
> I will fear no evil;
> For You are with me;
> Your rod and Your staff, they comfort me.
>
> Psalm 23:4 (NKJV)

When our hearts are in tune with God's will our soul can have restful assurance that He is with us through every trial and distressing situation. We do not know why we must go "through the valley of the shadow of death" but know it is necessary at times. How we react to what we are going through is up to us and we need to realize "In the world you will have tribulation; but be of good cheer, I have overcome the world" (John 16:33 NKJV). David went through trials as we will also, and could look back when they were over and appreciate His loving hand and protection. Through these experiences we gain substance and character, as David did, and are made ready to fight the Goliath's that come into our paths. On this journey with Him, "in the hidden part You will make me to know wisdom" (Psalm 51:6 NKJV). This same wisdom that David spoke of was talked about by Paul in his prayer for the Ephesians, "the God of our Lord Jesus Christ, the Father of glory, may give to you the spirit of wisdom and revelation in the knowledge of Him" (Ephesians 1:17 NKJV).

> When a man's heart is right with God the mysterious utterances of the Bible are spirit and life to him. Spiritual truth is discernible only to a pure heart, not to a keen intellect. It is not a question of profundity of intellect, but of purity of heart.
>
> (Bringing Sons Unto Glory, Oswald Chambers)

Solomon commented in Proverbs 23:26 (NKJV): "My son, give me your heart, and let your eyes observe my ways." A. B. Simpson in his "The Christ in the Bible Commentary" writes of what our heart receives after we give our heart to Him:

> When He comes to abide within us He simply imparts to us His own nature and Spirit, and puts into our heart the very same sentiments of trust toward His Father which He Himself ever cherished. There is nothing so delightful as this consciousness of the very life and heart of Christ within us, the trust that springs spontaneously within our breast, the prayer that prays itself, and the song that sings in joyous triumph even when all around is dark and strange.

The supreme importance for us as it was for David, was to "love the Lord your God with all your heart, with all your soul, and with all your mind" (Matthew 22:37 NKJV). When we come to God with a "broken and a contrite heart" (Psalm 51:17 NKJV) as David did, God has achieved His purpose in us, the battle for our heart has been won. "The author and finisher of our faith" (Hebrews 12:2 NKJV) has obtained guilt free believers because their sins have been dealt with and they are willing to "do all My will" (Acts 13:22 NKJV), for "His names sake" (Psalm 23:3 NKJV).

CPSIA information can be obtained
at www.ICGtesting.com
Printed in the USA
FFOW02n1556180118
44587690-44472FF